*The Tale of Thorstein Staff-Struck* is a short saga set in Iceland's East Fjords during the Viking Age. Thorstein, a peaceful young man, is struck in the course of a horse fight by an opponent wielding a wooden staff used as a horse-prod. From then on, Thorstein is mocked and forced to live with the humiliating nickname "staff-struck." Even Thorstein's father, an old viking, looks down on his son as a coward.

But Thorstein is no coward. Waiting for the right moment to take revenge, he reclaims his good name in a way that brings honor to both him and his chieftain. This new English translation is a dual language edition that includes the complete Old Norse text with full vocabulary and notes. The combination provides the tools needed to read a saga in English and Old Norse.

For more about Icelandic sagas, Old Norse, and the Viking Age
Visit our website: www.oldnorse.org

## About the Contributors to this Edition of the *Tale of Thorstein Staff-Struck*

Jesse Byock is distinguished research professor of Old Norse and Medieval Scandinavian at the University of California, Los Angeles (UCLA) specializing in the Viking World, its sagas, history, and archaeology. He is a professor at the UCLA Cotsen Institute of Archaeology. He studied in France, Iceland, and Sweden and earned his Ph.D. from Harvard University. In Iceland, he directs the Mosfell Archaeological Project (MAP) and is a professor at the University of Iceland (Háskóli Íslands) in the Department of History and the Programs of Medieval Icelandic and Viking Studies. He is the author of *Viking Age Iceland, Feud in the Icelandic Sagas,* and numerous articles and saga translations.

Randall Gordon is a specialist in historical linguistics of Celtic and Germanic Languages with concentrations on the development and grammar of Old Norse and Old Irish. He received his Ph.D. in Indo-European Studies from UCLA.

Ármann Jakobsson is professor of medieval Icelandic literature at the University of Iceland (Háskóli Íslands). He specializes in sagas, medieval literature, cultural studies, and folklore. He is the author of many books and articles including studies of J.R.R. Tolkien and Old Norse mythic elements.

# The Tale of Thorstein Staff-Struck
## (*Þorsteins þáttr stangarhöggs*)

## A New English Translation with Old Norse Text, Vocabulary, and Notes

by
Jesse Byock and Randall Gordon

Introduction by
Ármann Jakobsson and Jesse Byock

A Volume in the
Viking Language Old Norse Icelandic Series

www.oldnorse.org
www.juleswilliampress.com

Jules William Press
www.oldnorse.org
www.juleswilliampress.com

*The Tale of Thorstein Staff-Struck (Þorsteins þáttr stangarhöggs): A New English Translation with Old Norse Text, Vocabulary, and Notes*



ISBN: 978-1-953947-14-7

Cover design by Basil Arnould Price.
Cover image of Jelling II runestone (10th century AD). Tracing by Libbe Sambiria Bjerknæs (https://making-humanity.org/image/jelling-stone/, Creative Commons Attribution-ShareAlike 4.0 International License); coloring, processing, and changes by Ilya V. Sverdlov (Creative Commons Attribution-ShareAlike 4.0 International License).

Printed in Cambria

Keywords: Old Norse, Old Icelandic; Icelandic saga, Icelandic, Viking, Scandinavia, feud, grammar, Viking language, language study

# PREFACE

## THIS BILINGUAL SAGA EDITION

This saga edition is a new English translation in a dual-language format with annotations and notes. The volume offers all the tools necessary to read a complete saga in both English and the original Old Norse. Each chapter contains a specific vocabulary of Old Norse words and phrases. A full vocabulary is found at the rear of the book, removing the need to consult outside dictionaries. This combination of English translation, original Old Norse text, and targeted Old Norse vocabulary is supplemented with maps, notes, and cultural sections. Together these elements allow the reader to explore the language, subtleties, and wonders of a saga about early Iceland's feuding society.

The Sagas of the East Fjords, from which the *Tale of Thorstein Staff-Struck* is drawn, are extraordinary medieval narratives, and this edition is an example of textual archaeology. It unearths and rediscovers an important but neglected saga text, recounting the lives of people in Weapon's Fjord (Vápnafjǫrðr) a thousand years ago. www.oldnorse.org

## THE MOST FREQUENT WORDS IN THE SAGAS

Word frequency is a key to learning Old Norse, and this saga volume in the *Viking Language Old Norse Icelandic Series* is designed around a word-frequency learning strategy. The symbol ❖ in the Vocabulary marks the 246 most frequent words found in the sagas. *Thorstein's Tale* is an ideal text for this learning method, because it incorporates many of these most frequent words.

These 246 words make up more than 80 percent of all words in the family sagas, and we recommend concentrating on these words when learning Old Norse. For a full listing of these most common 246 words, see the "Word Frequency Section" in Chapter 1 of *Viking Language 1: Learn Old Norse, Runes and Icelandic Sagas* (Jules William Press) and in Appendix 2 ("Word Frequency") of the same volume.

## TABLE OF CONTENTS



## TABLE OF FIGURES

# INTRODUCTION

Ármann Jakobsson and Jesse Byock

*Are you not now becoming like those women who bemoan at one moment what they incite at another? I have too long endured taunts of cowardice from both you and others. It is of no avail to deter me when I am determined to go.*

–The chieftain Bjarni to his wife Rannveig

The *Tale of Thorstein Staff-Struck* (*Þorsteins þáttr stangarhǫggs*) is a *þáttr*, an Icelandic literary or historical term meaning a 'tale', 'short story', 'short saga', or 'episode.'[1] This *tháttr* might better be named *Þorsteins saga stangarhǫggs* (the *Saga of Thorstein Staff-Struck*), as a short saga it recounts a full story of insult, revenge, and honor among immediate descendants of the first 9th-and early 10th-century settlers to Iceland.

As a story about Icelanders in the 10th- and early 11th-centuries, *Thorstein's Tale* or *Saga* belongs to the group of Icelandic medieval writings called the family sagas or *Íslendingasögur* ('Sagas of the Icelanders'). The story was probably first written down in the 12th or 13th century and is set in Iceland during the 10th-century Viking Age. The violence of the Viking Period is never distant, and the tale opens with the mention of Thorstein's father Thorarin, an old viking introduced in the following way:

> There was a man named Thorarin, who lived in Sunnudal. He was an old man and poor of eyesight. He had been a red viking [*rauðavíkingr*, a fierce viking] in his youth and was not an agreeable man even when he was old.

Throughout history, the East Fjords have been among the most unknown regions of Iceland in the public imagination. Often shown on the 17th-century early maps of Iceland as being much smaller than it actually is, the Eastern region has been less

---

1 *Þáttr* physically means a 'strand' of rope or yarn.

prominent over time than the North, West, and South. As a distinct region, the East Fjords remained somewhat isolated until

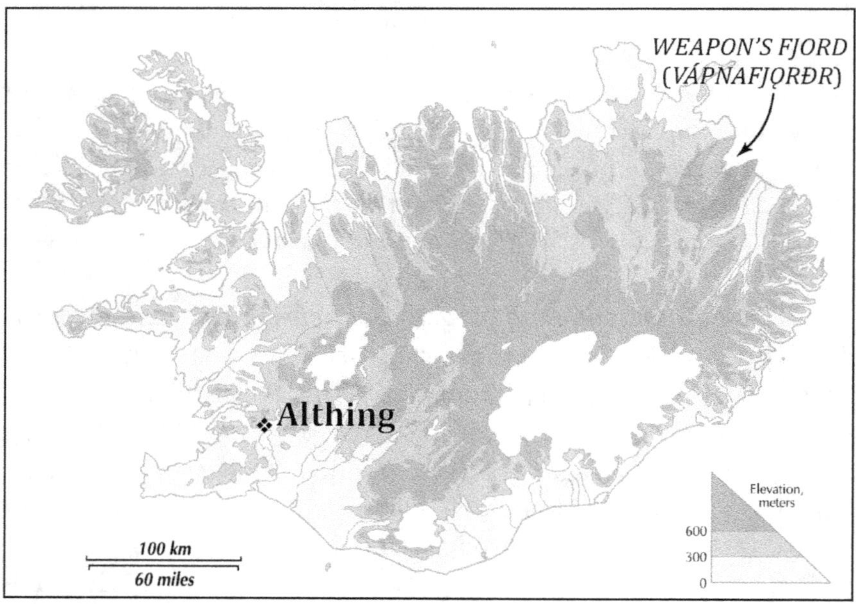


**Figure 1. The *Tale of Thorstein Staff-Struck*** takes place in Weapon's Fjord (Vápnafjǫrðr), a region in Iceland's East Fjords. Weapon's Fjord was first settled in the 9th century during the Viking Age and took its name from one of the first settlers, a *landnámsmaðr* or 'land-taking man' named Eyvind the Weapon (Eyvindr Vápni). The Old Norse term *fjǫrðr* ('fjord') includes the coastal region and the connected inland, lowland valley. These valleys were often well watered and fertile. The coast offered access to rich ocean fisheries. The families of chieftains (*goðar*) tended to control the best valley lands and coastal areas, while free farmers and tenant farmers often lived in the narrow side valleys, where they maintained modest farms and raised small herds of sheep and cattle. Some freemen, such as Thorstein Staff-Struck and Thorarin, his old father, made their living by breeding horses.

the late 20th century, in part because the modern ring road around Iceland that connects the East Fjords with the rest of the country was not completed until 1975.

If the East Fjords were fairly distant and mysterious, they have played a significant role within saga literature. A collection of important medieval texts from this region is known as the *Sagas of the East Fjords* (*Austfirðinga sögur*),[2] and the *Tale of Thorstein Staff-Struck* is prominent among these. The written version of this lively narrative has been dated to the mid-13th century, and it is frequently presented as a short saga within the corpus of the family sagas. For example, the Icelandic historian Jón Jóhannesson refers to the *Tale of Thorstein Staff-Struck* as a "*smásaga*" ('small saga') in his *Íslenzk fornrit* edition of the Sagas of the East Fjords.

Lying far off and uninhabited in the North Atlantic, Iceland (*Ísland* in Old Norse) was given its name by the first 9th-century Norse seamen, walrus hunters, and explorers who sighted its glaciers and were tested by its long winters. Except for the presence of a few Irish monks, who had arrived earlier seeking solitude, and who soon departed or 'disappeared', the Norse settlers to Iceland did not have to contend with a native population. This meant that over a period of decades the settlers took the best land.

Called *landnámsmenn* or 'landtakers' (a term that includes women), these first Viking Age settlers are memorialized in Iceland's sagas and medieval historical writings. *Landnámsmenn* had with them family, retainers, free laborers, and slaves. There were some Celts among them, especially women, but the dominant language was West Norse, the Old Scandinavian language of Viking Age Norway. This variant of Old Norse became the language of Iceland and the Old Icelandic of the sagas.[3]

The East Fjords formed, then as now, a distinct region. The 'landtakers' who led the migration to these distant fjords and inland valleys were free farmers in their home lands. Some were members of leading families, and a significant number came from Viking outposts in the British Isles. Most had ties to Norway. These first settlers brought with them the warlike culture of Viking Age Scandinavia and left it to their descendants to sort out

---

2 Jón Jóhannesson, ed. *Austfirðinga sǫgur*. Reykjavík: Hið íslenzka fornritafélag, 1950.

3 East Norse was the language of the Scandinavian regions of the Baltic.

for themselves the means for learning how to live with each other in Iceland's feud-rich society. In many ways, this search is what *Thorstein's Tale* is about. Events turn on the need to reconcile insults and killings among the second and third generations of Icelanders born in Weapon's Fjord.

The roots of the compositional technique in stories such as *Thorstein's Tale* are deeply set in the feuding traditions of medieval Icelanders. Many of these culturally oriented traditions were inherited from the Scandinavian homelands and were shaped in the 10th century by the island's evolving social, judicial, and governmental forms. Unlike the kingdoms, earldoms, and large-scale chieftaincies that the settlers left behind, early Icelanders created in their new home a society based on the rights of freemen.

Conflicts in the family sagas, unlike European epic struggles, are not contests between men and monsters, demons, or foreign or pagan forces. They do not decide the safety or the destruction of a people or a nation, and most epics deal with heroes on whom the society depends in the event of attack. or dangers to society. In contrast, Iceland's sagas are primarily about disputes between ordinary people over ordinary matters.

Feud on the island was more a public than a private matter, and for the most part, as we see in *Thorstein's Tale*, the violence involved Iceland's small-scale chieftains, the *goðar* (sing, *goði*) and the local farmers, the *bœndr* (sing. *bóndi*).[4] We suggest that the *Tale of Thorstein Staff-Struck* be read together with the *Saga of the People of Weapon's Fjord. Vápnfirðinga saga* is unapologetically rough and straightforward about bloodfeud as

---

[4] In early Iceland, the *goðar* were more like local 'big men' or political leaders than the warrior chieftains of many contemporary northern European cultures. *Goðar*, both as individuals and as a group, had only limited ability to control the free landowning farmers (*bœndur*). Bjarni in the *Tale of Thorstein Staff-Struck* is an example of a *goði* functioning as a local big man. Although not a commanding nobility, *goðar* functioned as leaders of interest groups composed of followers, called thingmen, drawn from among the farmers. The different *goðar* in a region often competed for the allegiance of the surrounding *bœndur*.

its primary focus. Together these two texts offer a full range of the issues and passions that motivate saga telling. Taken

**Figure 2. Horse Fights.** The feud in *Thorstein's Tale* begins at a horse fight. Called a *hestavíg*, *hestaat*, or *hestaþing*, horse fights were a common sport in early Iceland during the Viking and Medieval periods. In each contest two stallions (*hestar*, sing *hestr*) fought each other egged on by their masters. Horse fights are mentioned in numerous sagas, including *Njal's Saga*, *Viga-Glums Saga*, *Grettir's Saga*, *Eyrbyggja Saga*, *Kormac's Saga*, and *Reykdæla Saga*. These pictures were taken in 1930 at the Althing at Thingvellir (Þingvellir). The competition was staged during the 1000-year anniversary celebration of the Althing (930-1930) as part of an attempt to revive the tradition of horse fighting. The attempt failed. One can judge the size of the Icelandic horses by the men in the picture (Photo by the Swedish archaeologist Berit Wallenberg, 1930, Swedish National Heritage Board).

together, they describe different aspects of a distant, self-sufficient North Atlantic community struggling with the need to keep the peace in the face of conflicting calls for honor, vengeance, and demands of bloodfeud.

Almost anything can start a saga feud. Quarrels begin over contested landownership, insults, concepts of honor, inheritance matters, disputed dowries, and rejected love. Sources of subsistence, including control over hayfields and beached whales (a great source of meat and fat) or the right to remain in peace on one's land come into play. Containing conflict is also a main theme in the sagas. Often, as in the case in *Thorstein's Tale*, the characters live close to each other.

Thorstein's *Tale* can be characterized in various ways, but at heart, it is a realistic-sounding prose narrative offering insight into the lives and struggles of men and women who lived a thousand years ago in Weapon's Fjord. If it were not for saga telling and Iceland's other medieval writings, we would know nothing about Thorstein and his horse fight. We can assume that the original saga audience included the local people, and in the *Tale,* reference is made to prevailing opinions in the district.

The community described in *Thorstein's Tale* is a microcosm that represents the macrocosm of Old Icelandic feuding and social relations. Two families and farms feature prominently (see the map, Figure 4). One is Hof, the estate of Bjarni Brodd-Helgason.[5] The other is Thorstein Staff-Struck's small farm in Sunnudal (South Dale), a small side-valley to the inland fjord region of Weapon's Fjord. The chieftain or *goði* Bjarni lives at Hof with his wife Rannveig. In Bjarni's household at Hof are the trouble-making hired hands Thord, Thorhall, and Thorvald. The actions of these free laborers cause stir animosities. As individuals, they are aggressive braggarts, loud and obnoxious. These servants are overly proud that their *húsbóndi* (Bjarni, the master of their household) is a celebrated warrior.

Bjarni and Thorstein are of different social status. Bjarni is the son of the chieftain Brodd-Helgi. Like his father, Bjarni is himself a chieftain. Thorstein is a modest free farmer, and the tale makes

[5] Brodd-Helgi, is one of the main characters in the *Saga of the Families of Weapon's Fjord*. Thorarin is known only from *Thorstein's Tale*. There is, however, a man named Thorarin, who is mentioned briefly in *Vápnfirðinga saga*, and he might be Thorstein's father.

much of this uneven relationship. Despite Thorstein's poverty, his free-farmer status as a land-owning *bóndi* gives him full legal rights, a factor that Bjarni is well aware of. Thorstein makes a meager but honorable living as a horse breeder. The saga describes Thorstein and his father Thorarin in the following manner:

> Thorstein was a big, powerful, even-tempered man, and he worked so hard on his father's farm that the work of three men would not have been more effective. Thorarin was a rather poor man, but he owned a good many weapons. Father and son also owned stud-horses. Selling stallions was their main source of income, for none of his horses fell short in either performance or temperament.

The inhabitants of Hof also include an unnamed man and woman. These chorus-like characters appear briefly in the story and can be interpreted as the voice of public opinion. Meanwhile, Thorstein lives simply on his farm in Sunndal and looks after his half-blind and bedridden old father Thorarin, the old viking. Despite being old and weak, Thorarin remains a fighter at heart for whom blood vengeance is a badge of honor.

All the women in *Thorstein's Tale* live in Bjarni's household, where they play short but important roles. Sometimes, women diminish violence. For instance, after killing Thord (Þórðr, one of Bjarni's men), Thorstein goes to the chieftain's farmstead at Hof to announce his killing as required by law. Walking into the chieftain's longhouse and announcing that he had just killed one of Bjarni's men could have been be a death trap. However, before reaching the longhouse, Thorstein meets an anonymous woman. Thorstein seizes the opportunity and asks the woman to tell Bjarni that a bull has gored Thord.

The woman responds to Thorstein that she will do so but will use her own discretion as to when. Only after time has passed and Thorstein is safely away does she make an announcement in the longhouse. Suddenly she remembers Thorstein's message and claims in the saga passage below that she did not want to awaken

Bjarni. Note the metaphorical language used to describe the violence of feud.

> Thorstein Staff-Struck came here this morning and said that a bull had gored Thord so that he was unable to help himself. But I did not want to waken you, and afterward it slipped my mind (Chapter 2).

Acting as her own agent, the nameless woman elects neither to awaken Bjarni immediately nor to hide the fact that Thorstein did the killing. In some ways, we can see her as a "middle man," a successful tactician who cleverly avoids reporting the slaying in

**Hestaat í Bolabás.**

**Figure 3. Horse fights (continued).** Icelandic Horses are related to tough Mongolian horses. Although short-legged, Icelandic stallions are muscular and powerful. A *hestaþing*, as such a contest is called in the *Tale of Thorstein Staff-Struck*, meant a 'thing' or assembly-meeting for a public horse-fight. Icelandic stallions are known to be fierce fighters. After the unsuccessful attempt to revive horse-fighting in the 1930s, the practice died out in modern Iceland (Photo by Berit Wallenberg, 1930, Swedish National Heritage Board) .

order to delay further bloodshed. At this point the saga is a good example of saga narrative. While the woman provides comic relief between moments of tension, Thorstein is himself making a play on words when he says "*at naut hafi* ***stangat*** *Þór*'" ('that an ox has gored Thord'). Here Thorstein is playing with his nickname ***stangar****hǫgg* ('staff-struck'), but he is reversing the roles. Thorstein is now on the giving end rather than the receiving end. He is the ox who has ***stangat*** ('gored') the man responsible for striking him and giving him his derisive nickname.[6]

At another point in the tale, Bjarni's wife Rannveig attempts to goad her husband into seeking vengeance. Thorstein has publicly humiliated Bjarni by killing two of the chieftain's men. Rannveig, aware that her husband is not just a *goði* but also a skilled fighter, shames Bjarni by telling him that the district is abuzz about Thorstein's getting away with the killings. Rannveig worries that Bjarni will not only lose his honor but also his supporters at the annual Althing assembly.

Bjarni, however, views the ethics of the situation somewhat differently. In fine saga style, terse and to the point, we see the situation through Rannveig's eyes and through Bjarni's:

> In the morning, Rannveig woke as Bjarni was taking down his shield. She asked where he intended to go.
>
> He answered: "There will now be an exchange of honor between Thorstein and me at Sunnudal."
>
> "How many men are you going to take with you?" she asked.
>
> "I will not drag a crowd against Thorstein," he said. "I shall go alone."

Rannveig, realizing the result of her goading, quickly changes her tune. She pleads with her husband not to go alone but to take a following of men with him so that he does not risk his own life. At this point Bjarni's patience runs out. He makes an impassioned

---

[6] There is similar imagery in *Vápnfirðinga saga*, where feuding men of the district appear in a prophetic dream as *naut* 'oxen'. In this dream, the chieftain Bjarni is represented as 'a red ox with bone-colored horns, and, of all oxen, the most splendid' (*rauðr uxi, ok var beinlitr á hornunum, ok var allra nauta skrautligastr*). The oxen rose up at Hof and gored (*stangaði*) to death his (Bjarni's) father's killer.

speech about the incitements of women, who first clamor for blood, but then try to stop their men.

In general, the characters in the story can be divided into two categories. On the one hand there are the mature farmers, Bjarni and Thorstein. On the other hand, there are women, workers, and elderly, that is everybody else. In general, the characters split between those who fight and those who incite others. This opposition is a catalyst in the story and epitomises two attitudes toward the violence of Iceland's feuding culture. Within this opposition we see that one group at first sight is perceived as weaker, but can hold the other hostage through efficient management of public opinion. Intertwined within this dynamic are constant calls for upholding codes of honor.

Consider more closely the steps in the escalating conflict. Bjarni's stableman Thord is the antagonist who initiated the conflict. Thord, who is introduced in the tale as an "*ójafnaðarmaðr mikill*" (an 'aggressively overbearing man') finds his chance to bully by challenging Thorstein to a horse fight. Once in the contest, Thord loses his composure. In order to help his stallion gain the upper hand, Thord strikes Thorstein's horse with his horse prod (a stout wooden stick). Thorstein retaliates by striking Thord's horse. Then Thord uses his prod to hit Thorstein in the face above the eye. The wound draws blood.

Although having been struck in public, Thorstein chooses not to seek revenge immediately. Still, the blow is the beginning of a deadly conflict. Two of Bjarni's hired hands, Thorvald and Thorhall, insult Thorstein and give him the nickname, "*stangarhǫgg*" ('staff-struck'). In the saga world, there is a strong correlation between nicknames and mocking, and this instance of mockery offers a glimpse into ethics and shaming in early Iceland.

In the sagas, which retain many aspects of Viking Age culture, a blow drawing blood was an act of dishonor to the victim. Consider for instance *Njal's Saga*, where Gunnar from Hlíðarendi (Slope's End) is accidently hit by a horse and then ridiculed by opponents who claim that he wept. Such a blow, magnified by the ridicule of the accusation, required the injured party to seek vengeance for the insult. As a consequence, men died. The *Tale of Thorstein Staff-Struck* adds the issue that some men and women clamor for revenge but want to do so without endangering themselves or their people.

Thorstein's story was likely not conceived as a strictly independent tale but as part of a collection of sagas about people and events in the East Fjords. Signs of this connection can be seen in text of *Thorstein's Tale* in the first mention of the *goði* Bjarni Brodd-Helgason from Hof (*Bjarni frá Hofi*), where Bjarni is treated as if no introduction is needed.

Bjarni was called Víga-Bjarni (Killer-Bjarni) because of his success in bloodfeud, and he is most known for being one of the main characters in the *Saga of the People of Weapon's Fjord* (*Vápnfirðinga saga*),[7] and *Thorstein's Tale* appears to be one of a series of sagas and tales that complement *Vápnfirðinga saga*.[8] Bjarni's presence in both narratives links *Vápnfirðinga saga* with the *Tale* of *Thorstein Staff-Struck*, but Bjarni also makes appearances in *Njal's Saga*, *Fljótsdæla saga* and the *Short Saga of Gunnar, the Killer of Thidrandi* (*Gunnars þáttr Þiðrandabana*).

A hint about the dating of the tale's early manuscript is found at the very end of the story. There, the audience is provided with genealogies of prominent Icelandic magnates (*stórgoðar* or *stórhöfðinjar*, 'big leaders') from the first part of the 13th century.[9] This inclusion of 13th-century leaders seems to indicate that the roots of the written story lie in the Age of the Sturlungs (a period of civil unrest in 13thcentury Iceland), and that the tale's intended audience was familiar with personalities from that era.

---

[7] For a discussion of bloodfeud in the *Saga of the People of Weapon's Fjord*, see *Viking Age Iceland*, pp 233-251.

[8] The surviving text of the *Tale of Thorstein Staff-Struck* is named as 'an episode from *Vápnfirðinga saga*' in the 17th-century paper manuscript 496.

[9] These include famous leaders such as Þorvaldr (Thorvald) Gissurarson of Hruni (d. 1235), Magnús Guðmundsson (d. 1240), Digr-Helgi Þorsteinsson (Fat Helgi Thorsteinsson, d. 1235), the brothers Þórðr (Thord, d. 1237), Sighvatr (d. 1238) and Snorri Sturluson (d. 1241), and Ormr Jónsson Svínfellingr (d. 1241).

In light of dating the story to the 13th-century time of troubles, it is interesting to note that *Thorstein's Tale* explores discord and conflict that ends with a peaceful resolution. That a story of reconciliation could grow out of the violent atmosphere that characterized the Age of the Sturlungs indicates, perhaps, that the *Tale of Thorstein Staff-Struck* was aimed against the prevailing feuding ideals of vengeance seeking.

## Manuscripts

Thorstein Staff-Struck's story has survived in only a few manuscripts. One, a single vellum (skin) manuscript, AM 162 C fol., dates from the 15th century. This skin manuscript contains only one tightly written page of the tale, but over half the narrative is preserved on this page.

Beginning in the 16th century, inexpensive, blank paper books manufactured in Northern Europe where imported into Iceland. Icelanders used these blank books to copy texts from the older vellum manuscripts, which by that time had become aged and difficult to read. As a result, the medieval texts gained new life, and they appear to have been widely read. In this way, many sagas and *þættir* (plural of *þáttr*) were preserved, and the *Tale of Thorstein Staff-Struck* is one of these.

In its most complete form, *Þorsteins saga stangarhǫggs* is found in two paper manuscripts from the 17th century, AM 156 fol. and AM 496 4to. Both 17th-century paper manuscripts 156 and 162 are copies of fragments of a larger, probably older medieval vellum.

In all three surviving manuscripts, the *Tale of Thorstein Staff-Struck* is placed among other sagas from Iceland's East Fjords. The vellum manuscript 162 includes *Vápnfirðinga saga* (*Saga of the People of Weapon's Fjord*) and *Droplaugarsona saga* (*Saga of the Sons of Droplaug*). The paper manuscripts 156 and 496 contain *Hrafnkels saga Freysgoða* (*Hrafnkel's Saga, Priest of Frey*) and *Þorsteins saga hvíta* (*Saga of Thorstein the White*), along with other shorter narratives about the East Fjords.

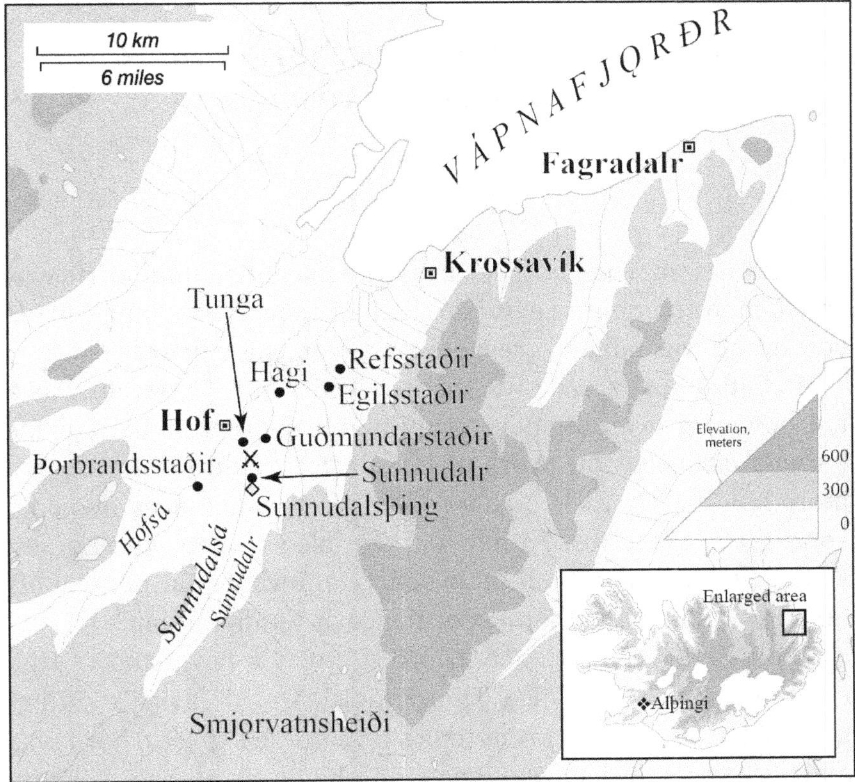


**Figure 4. Weapon's Fjord (Vápnafjǫrðr): The Landscape of the *Tale of Thorstein Staff-Struck*.** Thorstein, the main character in the tale, lived in Sunnudalr ('South Valley'), a small dale on the south side of the main fjord valley. Víga-Bjarni ('Killer Bjarni'), the other major character, was a chieftain living at Hof, the richest farmstead in Weapon's Fjord (Vápnafjǫrðr). Hof was the seat of Bjarni's family, the Hofverjar ('People of Hof'). From there, Bjarni controlled a wide swath of rich bottom lands. His holdings included a major salmon river, the Hof River (Hofsá). The map also shows the location of the Sunnudalsþing (the 'South Valley Assembly'), where local freemen and chieftains met annually. At the inland (eastern) end of Weapon's Fjord lies the vast highland heath called Smjǫrvatnsheiði ('Butter-Water Heath'). Bǫðvarsdalr ('Bodvar's Valley' or 'Bodvar's Dale'), up in the coastal mountains, was the site of the famous battle mentioned in this tale (for more on the battle, see the *Saga of the People of Weapon's Fjord*).

## *The Tale of Thorstein Staff-Struck*
### (English Translation)

# Chapter 1

There was a man named Thorarin, who lived in Sunnudal. He was an old man and poor of eyesight. He had been a red viking[10] in his youth, and was not an agreeable man even when he was old.

He had one son, who was named Thorstein. Thorstein was a big, powerful, even-tempered man, and he worked so hard on his father's farm that the work of three men would not have been more helpful. Thorarin was a rather poor man, but he owned a good many weapons. Father and son also owned stud-horses. Selling stallions was their main source of income, for none of his horses fell short in either performance or temperament.

There was a man named Thord. He was a farmhand of [the chieftain] Bjarni at Hof.[11] Thord took care of Bjarni's riding-horses, because he was reputed to be a horse expert. Thord was an exceedingly overbearing man, and he let many people know that he was the servant of a powerful man. But he himself was none- the-more-worthy for it, nor was he the-better-liked.

There were yet other men staying at Bjarni's. One was named Thorhall and another Thorvald. They were great gossips and repeated everything that they heard in the district.

Thorstein and Thord arranged a horse-fight for young stallions.[12] But when they egged the stallions on, Thord's horse

---

[10] **Red Viking**: *rauðavíkingr*, a fierce viking.

[11] The saga audience would have known that the reference was to Víga-Bjarni ('Killer Bjarni'), a famous warrior and chieftain (*goði*). Bjarni lived at the farmstead of Hof and plays an important role in this tale.

[12] Horse fighting, called *hesta-at* or *hesta-víg*, was a major form of entertainment. In this rough sport, stallions were pitted against each other, and the contests often led to violence among the men, who used wooden prods or staffs to urge on their horses.

was less eager to fight.[13] When Thord realized that his horse was faring worse, he struck Thorstein's horse on the muzzle with a great blow. But Thorstein saw that and in return struck Thord's horse with an even greater blow. And as Thord's horse fled, men cheered vigorously. Then Thord struck Thorstein on the brow with his horse-staff, so that the skin fell down over Thorstein's eye. Thorstein tore off part of his shirt and bound up his brow, and, acting as if nothing had happened, he requested that the men hide this incident from his father. The matter was then dropped.

Thorvald and Thorhall took this as an occasion for ridicule, and they called him Thorstein Staff-Struck.

## Chapter 2

In the winter shortly before Yule, the women at Sunnudal got up and began their work. Thorstein also got up and brought in the hay, and afterwards lay down on the bench. Then old Thorarin, his father, came in and asked who was lying there.[14] Thorstein identified himself.

"Why are you so early afoot, son?" asked old Thorarin.

Thorstein answered, "It seems to me that few others are fighting over what needs to be done here."

"Isn't your head injured, son?" asked old Thorarin.

"Not that I know of," said Thorstein.

"What do you have to say to me, son, about the horse fight that took place last summer? Were you not, kinsman, struck with a staff like a dog?"

"I don't think there is any honor," said Thorstein, "in calling it an intentional blow rather than an accident."

Thorarin said, "I would not have expected that I would have a cowardly son."

"Say about this now, father," said Thorstein, "only as much as you will not think overstated later."

---

[13] **fight:** *bítask*, literally 'bite each other'.

[14] Small turf buildings were dark inside, and Thorarin was nearly blind.

"I will not speak as much about it here," said Thorarin, "as I have a mind to."

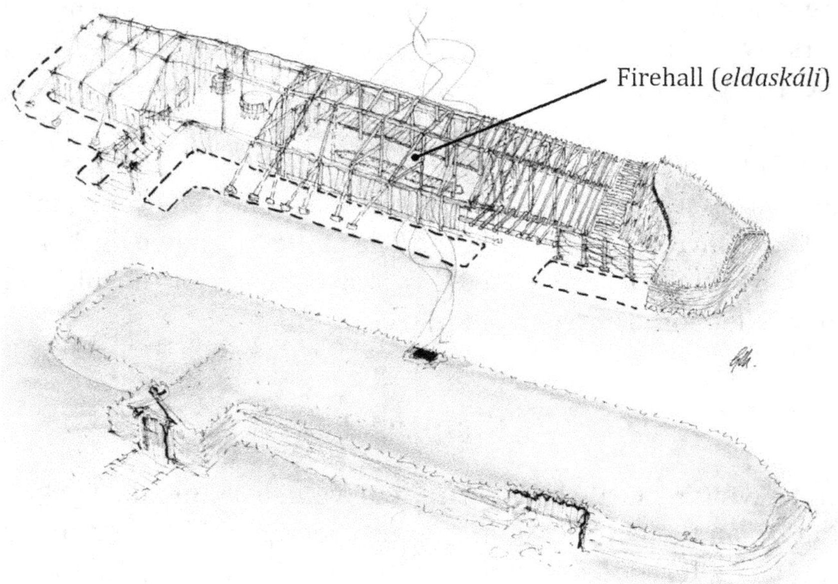


**Figure 5. A Chieftain's Longhouse**. The longhouse of Bjarni, the chieftain at Hof, would have been an imposing Viking Age turf structure similar to the one pictured here, which was excavated at Hrísbrú in the Mosfell Valley. The internal diagram shows the main living space, the firehall (*eldaskáli*), with its long fire running down the center of the floor. The wooden frame and wall partitions, including the interior wooden doors, were mostly made of driftwood collected along the coast. The thick turf walls and grass-covered roof insulated the structure, protecting it from the strong northern winds. The larger door to the right was for the milking cattle who spent the winter indoors. The longhouses of the chieftains were more spacious than the modest turf longhouse in which Thorstein and his father lived. (Drawing from - architectural studies of the Mosfell structures by Jesse Byock and Grétar Markússon, Mosfell Archaeological Project).

Then Thorstein got up. He took his weapon, left the house, and went to the stable where Thord tended Bjarni's horses. Thord was there.

Thorstein approached Thord and said to him, "I would like to know, Thord my friend, whether that blow I got from you last summer at the horse fight was accidental or if you did it on purpose, and whether you would be willing to compensate me for it."

Thord answered, "If you have two cheeks, then stick your tongue into each of them in turn and call it an accident in one, if you want, and in the other, call it something intentional. And that is all the compensation you are getting from me."

"Prepare yourself then," said Thorstein, "for it may be that I will not come to collect again."

Then Thorstein leapt at him and dealt Thord his death blow. Afterwards he went to the house at Hof, and finding one of the women outside, and said to her, "Tell Bjarni that an ox has gored Thord, his horse-boy, and Thord will be waiting there by the stable until he comes."

"Go on home, man," she said, "and I will tell him when it seems good to me."

Then Thorstein went home, and the woman went about her work.

Bjarni got up in the morning. When he came to the table, he asked where Thord was, and men answered that he would likely have gone to the horses.

"Yet I would have expected him to have come home by now," said Bjarni, "if he were well."

Then the woman whom Thorstein had happened to meet spoke up: "It is true what is often said to us women, that little intelligence is to be had where we women are concerned. Thorstein Staff-Struck came here this morning and said that a bull had gored Thord so that he was unable to help himself. But I did not want to waken you, and afterward it slipped my mind."

Then Bjarni got up from the table, went to the stable and there found Thord killed. Thord was buried afterwards.

Bjarni then prepared a lawsuit and condemned Thorstein to outlawry for the killing. But Thorstein remained at home in Sunnudal working for his father, and Bjarni let everything lie quiet.

## Chapter 3

In the autumn, men were sitting around the roasting-fire at Hof, while Bjarni lay down outside the wall of the fire-house, from where he listened to the men's talk.

Now the brothers Thorhall and Thorvald spoke up: "We did not expect, when we took up lodging with Killer-Bjarni,[15] that we would be roasting lambs' heads[16] here while Thorstein, his outlaw, should be roasting geldings' heads.[17] Would it not have been better if he had spared his own kinsmen in the Battle at Bodvarsdal,[18] than to have this outlaw sitting as an equal to him in Sunnudal? But those who are struck despair when facing wounds.[19] And we do not know when Bjarni will want to wipe this stain from his honor."

One man answered, "That kind of thing is worse said than kept silent. Likely trolls have drawn the tongue out of your head.[20] We

---

[15] Bjarni was the son of the overbearing chieftain Brodd-Helgi Thorgilsson, whose slaying is recounted in *Vápnfirðinga saga*. Barni was called Víga-Bjarni ('Killer-Bjarni') because of his revenge killings for the death of his father. Along with his role in Thorstein's tale and *Vápnfirðinga saga*, Víga-Bjarni is mentioned in several other Icelandic sources, including *Landnámabók* (*The Book of Settlements*).

[16] Sheep's heads were roasted over open fires in the autumn. Singed black by the fire, the heads were (and are still today) considered a delicacy. The blackened heads are at times mentioned in sagas and poetry.

[17] The meaning here is that Bjarni's outlaw (Thorstein Staff-Struck) is enjoying more freedom than Bjarni's own servants.

[18] These events are described in *Vápnfirðinga saga*. The passage suggests that the readers (or hearers) of *Þorsteins þáttr stangarhǫggs* would have been familiar with *Vápnfirðinga saga*. Bodvarsdal is the valley where Bjarni successfully fought his kinsman (cousin) and rival chieftain, Thorkel Geitisson.

[19] **Those who are struck despair when facing wounds:** *Lagðir verða forlagðir, ef fyrir sárunum verða*, an obscurb proverb that does not occur in any other saga. The two brothers are accusing Bjarni of losing his courage in the face of the possibility of being wounded by Thorstein.

[20] Meaning that these foolish words were uttered under the influence of trolls.

suppose that he is not inclined to deprive the man's sightless father and those other dependent folk at Sunnudal of their subsistence. But it will surprise me, if you roast lambs' heads here much longer or gloat over what occurred at Bodvarsdal."[21]

Then the men went to eat and afterwards to sleep, and Bjarni gave no sign of having heard what had been said.

In the morning Bjarni woke Thorhall and Thorvald. He told them to ride to Sunnudal and bring him Thorstein's head removed from its trunk by breakfast-time. "For you two seem to me," he said, "the likeliest ones to remove a stain from my honor, if I have no courage for it myself."

Now they knew for sure that they had said too much, but nonetheless they left and came to Sunnudal. Thorstein was standing in the doorway whetting a short sword.[22]

When they arrived, Thorstein asked where they were going. They said that they were supposed to be looking for some horses. Thorstein told them they would not have far to look – "since here they are by the yard."

"We aren't sure we will find the horses if you don't point them out to us more clearly."

So Thorstein went outside. And when they had come down into the yard, Thorvald raised his axe and leapt at Thorstein. But Thorstein shoved him with his hand so that Thorvald fell forward, and Thorstein thrust his short sword through him. Then Thorhall tried to make an assault on him, and fared the same as Thorvald.

Thorstein then tied them both on horseback. He set the reins up on the horses' necks and sent them all on their way, and the horses went home to Hof.

Some farmhands were outside at Hof. They went in and told Bjarni that Thorvald and Thorhall had come home, and that their errand had not been unsuccessful. Bjarni went out and saw how matters stood. He had nothing more to say about it, but he had them buried. Everything now remained quiet until Yule passed.

---

[21] See footnotes 15 and 18.

[22] **short sword:** *sax*, a common weapon. It usually had a wooden haft and most often was single-edged, sometimes with a curved blade. The *handsax* was a double-edged weapon.

## Chapter 4

Then one evening Rannveig[23] said, when Bjarni and she were going to bed, "What do you think is most talked about now in the district?"

"I don't know," said Bjarni. "I think many people are off the mark in what they say."

"What is now most widely gossiped about is that people cannot imagine what Thorstein Staff-Struck will have to do before you think it necessary to seek redress. He has now killed three of your farmhands. Your thingmen do not think they can count on support in matters where you are concerned, while this remains unavenged. Wrongly do your hands lie idle in your lap."

Bjarni answered, "Now we come to the point. It is just as the saying goes: no one takes another's punishment as warning. But I will listen to what you say, though few that Thorstein has killed were innocent."

They ended this talk and slept through the night.

In the morning, Rannveig woke as Bjarni was taking down his shield. She asked where he intended to go.

He answered, "There will now be an exchange of honor between Thorstein and me at Sunnudal."

"How many men are you going to take with you?" she asked.

"I will not draw a crowd against Thorstein," he said. "I shall go alone."

"Don't do it," she said. "Don't risk your life alone against the weapons of this powerful man-of-Hel."[24]

Bjarni replied, "Are you not now becoming like those women who bemoan at one moment what they incite at another? I have too long endured taunts of cowardice from both you and others. It is of no avail to deter me when I am determined to go."

---

[23] Rannveig Thorgeirsdottir, Bjarni's wife.

[24] **powerful man-of-Hel:** *heljarmaðr*, a 'powerful, rough man'. The term might also be translated as 'fiend from Hel'. *Hel*, cognate with English 'hell', is the abode of the dead, and also the name of the goddess of death.

# Chapter 5

Bjarni then went to Sunnudal. Thorstein was standing in the doorway, and they exchanged a few words.

Bjarni declared, "You must fight me in single combat today, Thorstein, on this hill here in the field."

"I have absolutely no desire," said Thorstein, "to fight with you. But I will go abroad as soon as ships are ready to sail, and I know your noble-mindedness is such that you will give my father farm help if I leave."

"There is no use now trying to talk your way out from under this," said Bjarni.

"Will you then allow me to go see my father first?" said Thorstein.

"Of course," said Bjarni.

Thorstein went inside and told his father that Bjarni had come there and challenged him to single combat.

Old Thorarin answered, "Every man can be sure to expect, if he has dealings with a more powerful man and dwells in the same district with him, and has also done him some dishonor, that he will not live to wear out many shirts. And I cannot mourn for you, because to me it seems that you have done a great deed. Take your weapons now and defend yourself as bravely as possible. Because in my time, I would not have bowed before such a man as Bjarni, although he is the greatest champion. It seems better to me to lose you than to have a cowardly son."

Thorstein went outside again. Then they went out onto the hill and began to fight boldly, and each hacked away much of the other's shield.

And when they had fought long and hard, Bjarni said to Thorstein, "I am thirsty now, for I am less used to exertion than you."

"Go to the brook then," said Thorstein, "and drink."

Bjarni did so and laid his sword down near him.

Thorstein picked it up, looked at it, and said, "You must not have had this sword at Bodvarsdal."

Bjarni answered nothing.

They then went up onto the hill and fought for a while. To Bjarni it seemed that the man who opposed him was skilled in fighting and better at it than he had expected.

"A lot of things are overtaking me today," said Bjarni. "Now my shoelace is loose."

"Tie it then," said Thorstein.

Then Bjarni bent down, and Thorstein went inside and brought out two shields and one sword.[25] He went to Bjarni on the hill and said to him, "Here is a shield and a sword which my father sent you, and this one will not grow blunt with the blows any more than the one that you have already. I also don't desire to stand unprotected any longer under your blows. But I would rather end this game now, because I am afraid that your good luck will avail more than my bad luck. And everyone is eager to survive through every struggle, if I might somehow get to decide this."

"It's no use to beg off now," said Bjarni. "You must fight on."

"I would not willingly strike," said Thorstein.

Then Bjarni struck the whole shield from Thorstein, whereupon Thorstein struck the shield from Bjarni.

"That was a great blow," said Bjarni.

Thorstein answered, "You did not strike a lesser blow."

Bjarni declared, "That same weapon that you have had since earlier today is biting better for you now."

Thorstein declared, "I would spare myself ill luck, if I might do so, and I am afraid to fight with you. I would still be willing to put everything in your power."

It was then Bjarni's turn to strike, and both were now without defense. Then Bjarni spoke: "It would be a bad bargain to choose a misdeed over great luck. I would consider myself to have been paid in full for my three household servants by you alone, if you

---

[25] For a shoe-lace tying that ends quite differently, consider Thorstein Egilsson's choice in *Egil's Saga* Chapter 81.

will be true to me."

Thorstein said, "I have had chance enough at you today that I could have betrayed you, if my misfortune had proved more powerful than your luck. I will not betray you."

"I see that you are an outstanding man," said Bjarni. "Will you allow me to go inside to your father and tell him what I wish?"

"Go as you like, for my part," said Thorstein. "But proceed warily."

## Chapter 6

Then Bjarni went to the bed-closet where old Thorarin was lying. Thorarin asked who was there, and Bjarni identified himself.

"What news do you have, Bjarni my friend?" asked Thorarin.

"The killing of Thorstein, your son," said Bjarni.

"Did he defend himself at all?" asked Thorarin.

"No one, I expect, has been quicker in battle than Thorstein your son."

"It's no wonder then," said the old man, "that you proved hard to deal with at Bodvarsdal, when now you have bested my son."

Then Bjarni said, "I wish to invite you to Hof. You shall sit in the second seat of honor as long as you live, and I will be in place of a son to you."

"It has turned out for me," said the old man, "the same as for those who have control over nothing. Only a foolish man takes delight in promises. And such are the promises of you chieftains, when you wish to comfort a man after incidents like this, that the relief lasts for a month. But after that our value is like any other pauper's, and our sorrows are slowly forgotten.

"However, he who shakes hands in bargain with a man like you can still be well content with his lot, whatever the outcome is. So I will accept your bargain. Come here to my bed-closet. And you must come near, for this old man is shaky on his feet because of age and poor health, nor is it likely that I am not affected by my son's death."

Bjarni went to the bed-closet and took old Thorarin's hand. Then he noticed that Thorarin was groping for a short sword and intended to attack him.

Bjarni pulled back his hand and exclaimed, "You most wretched old fart! Now our bargain will go the way you deserve. Thorstein your son is alive, and he is the one who will come home to Hof with me. But you will be given thralls for the farm work and shall lack for nothing as long as you live." Thorstein then went home to Hof with Bjarni and he supported Bjarni until the day of his death. And, Thorstein was considered a match for most anyone in courage and valor.

Bjarni fully maintained his honor, and he became better-liked and more even-tempered as he grew older. He was the most steadfast of men in difficulties. He became a great man of faith in the latter part of his life. Bjarni traveled abroad and went south,[26] and died on that trip. He lies in the town called Vateri, a big town not far this side of the city of Rome.[27]

Bjarni was a man blessed with many descendants. His son was Skegg-Broddi, who appears widely in sagas and was the most excellent of men in his day.[28] Bjarni's daughter was named Halla, the mother of Gudrid, whom Kolbein the Law-speaker married. Another of Bjarni's daughters was Yngvild, whom Thorstein Sidu-Hallsson married, and their son was Magnus, the father of Einar,

---

[26] On a pilgrimage to Rome.

[27] The town Vateri is unknown.

[28] Here the text refers to other sagas. While many sagas have been lost over the centuries, Bjarni's son Skegg-Broddi appears in the *Tale of Ale-Hood* (*Ǫlkofra þáttr*); the *Saga of Thorstein Sidu-Hallsson* (*Þorsteins saga Síðu-Hallssonar*); the *Saga of the People of Ljosavatn* (*Ljósvetninga saga*); and the *Saga of the Confederates* (*Bandamanna saga*). Beginning with Skegg-Broddi in the 10th century, the passage traces Bjarni's descendants, both men and women, down to prominent clerics, chieftains, and politicians in the 13th century, including: Kolbein Flosason, lawspeaker from 1066–1071; Magnus, bishop in Skalholt from 1134–1148; the Sturlusons; and another Magnus, a chieftain who was selected bishop in Skalholt in 1236 but was not consecrated because Icelanders at that time were denied the right to choose their own bishop. This Magnus drowned in 1240.

the father of Bishop Magnus. Another son of Thorstein and Yngvild was Amundi. He married Sigrid, the daughter of Thorgrim the Blind. Amundi's daughter was Hallfrid, the mother of Amundi, the father of Gudmund, the father of the chieftain Magnus and of Thora, whom Thorvald Gizurarson married, and of another Thora, the mother of Orm Svinfelling. Another daughter of Amundi was Gudrun, the mother of Thordis, the mother of Helga, the mother of Gudny Bodvarsdottir, the mother of the Sturlusons: Thord, Sighvat, and Snorri. Another daughter of Amundi was Rannveig, the mother of Stein, the father of Gudrun, the mother of Arnfrid, whom Stout-Helgi married. Another daughter of Amundi was Thorkatla, the mother of Arnbjorg, the mother of Finn the Priest, Thorgeir, and Thurid. And many magnificent men have come from them.

Here ends the tale of Thorstein Staff-Struck.

## *ÞORSTEINS ÞÁTTR STANGARHǪGGS*
### (OLD NORSE – ICELANDIC)

### 1. KAPÍTULI

Maðr hét Þórarinn, er bjó í Sunnudal, gamall maðr ok sjónlítill. Hann hafði verit rauðavíkingr í œsku sinni. Hann var eigi dældarmaðr, þótt hann væri gamall.

Son átti sér einn, er Þorsteinn er nefndr. Hann var mikill maðr ok ǫflugr ok vel stilltr ok vann svá fyrir búi fǫður síns, at eigi mundi þriggja verk manna annarra hallkvæmara.[29] Þórarinn var heldr félítill maðr, en vel margt átti hann vápna. Þeir áttu ok stóðhross feðgar, ok var þeim þat helzt til fjár, er þeir seldu undan hestana, því at engir brugðusk at reið né hug.[30]

Þórðr er maðr nefndr. Hann var húskarl Bjarna frá Hofi. Hann varðveitti reiðhesta Bjarna, því at hann var kallaðr hrossamaðr. Þórðr var ójafnaðarmaðr mikill, ok lét hann marga þess ok kenna, er hann var ríkismanns húskarl.[31] En eigi var hann sjálfr at meira verðr, ok eigi varð hann at vinsælli.[32]

Þeir menn váru enn á vist með Bjarna, er annarr hét Þórhallr, en annarr Þorvaldr. Þeir váru uppaustrarmenn miklir um allt þat, er þeir heyrðu í heraði.

---

[29] **vann svá fyrir búi fǫður síns, at eigi mundi þriggja verk manna annarra hallkvæmara:** 'he worked in such a way for his father's farmstead that the work of three men would not have been more helpful (or advantageous)'.

[30] **var þeim þat helzt til fjár, er þeir seldu undan hestana, því at engir brugðusk at reið né hug:** 'selling off stallions was their main source of income, for none of them (i.e., the horses) was a disappointment in performance (riding) or temperment'.

[31] **lét hann marga þess ok kenna, er hann var ríkismanns húskarl:** 'he also let many know that he was the servant of a powerful man'.

[32] **eigi var hann sjálfr at meira verðr, ok eigi varð hann at vinsælli:** 'he himself was none the more worthy (for it), and he did not become better-liked'.

Þeir Þorsteinn ok Þórðr mæltu til hestaats ungum hestum.[33] Ok er þeir ǫttu, þá vildi hestr Þórðar verr bítask. Þórðr lýstr nú á skoltinn hesti Þorsteins, er honum þótti sinn hestr verr hafa, mikit hǫgg. En Þorsteinn sá þat ok lýstr á móti hest Þórðar heldr meira hǫgg, ok rann nú hestrinn Þórðar, ok œpðu menn þá með kappi. Þá lýstr Þórðr Þorstein með hestastafnum, ok kom á brúnina, ok hljóp hon ofan fyrir augat. Þá risti Þorsteinn af skyrtublaði sínu ok bindr upp brúnina ok lætr sem ekki hafi at orðit ok biðr, at menn leyni þessu fǫður hans. Ok fell þetta þar nú niðr.

Þeir Þorvaldr ok Þórhallr hǫfðu þetta fyrir kallsi[34] ok kǫlluðu hann Þorstein stangarhǫgg.

## VOCABULARY TO CHAPTER 1

**af** *prep* [*w dat*] off (of)
**allr** (ǫll, allt) *adj* all
**annarr** (ǫnnur, annat) *adj* other, another; **annarr ... annarr** *indef pron* the one ... the other
**at** *prep* [*w dat*] at, in; as to, with respect to; on account of, by reason of
**at** *conj* that; so that; **því at** because
**auga** *n* eye
**á** *prep* [*w acc*] on, onto (*motion*); [*w dat*] on, in, at (*location or time*)
**átti** *3sg past of* **eiga**
**biðja** (biðr; bað, báðu; beðinn) *vb* ask, request, bid
**binda** (bindr; batt, bundu; bundinn) *vb* bind, tie
**bíta** (bítr; beit, bitu; bitinn) *vb* bite; *refl* **bítask** bite each other, fight (*of horses*)
**Bjarni** *m* Bjarni (*personal name*)
**bjó** *3sg past of* **búa**
**blað** *n* leaf; skirt of a shirt or cloak
**bregða** (bregðr; brá, brugðu; brugðinn) *vb* [*w dat*] break off, leave off; give up; *refl* **bregðask** fail, fall short, disappoint,
**brún** *f* eyebrow
**bú** *n* home, house; farm, farmstead
**búa** (býr; bjó, bjoggu/bjuggu; búinn) *vb* live (in a place), dwell
**dalr** *m* valley, dale
**dæld** *f* gentleness

[33] **mæltu til hestaats ungum hestum:** 'they arranged a horse-fight for young horses'.

[34] **Þeir Þorvaldr ok Þórhallr hǫfðu þetta fyrir kallsi:** 'Thorvald and Thorhall made use of this (event) for mockery'.

**dældarmaðr** *m* gentle, easy man
**eiga** (á, eigu; átti; áttr) *vb* own, have (relatives)
**eigi** *adv* not
**einn** (ein, eitt) *num* one; *adj* a, an, a certain one
**ekki** *n indef pron* nothing (*see* **engi**)
**en** *conj* but; and (on the other hand)
**engi** (*n* ekki; *pl m* engir) *adj/indef pron* no, no one, none
**enn** *adv* yet, still
**er** *rel pron* who; *conj* when
**er** *3sg pres of* **vera**
**etja** (etr; atti, ǫttu; attr) *vb* [*w dat*] incite, egg on to fight
**faðir** (*acc/dat/gen* fǫður) *m* father
**falla** (fellr; fell, fellu; fallinn) *vb* fall; **falla niðr** be dropped, forgotten
**feðgar** *m pl* father and son(s)
**fell** *3sg past of* **falla**
**fé** (*gen* fjár) *n* property; money, wealth
**félítill** *adj* short of money, poor
**fjár** *gen sg of* **fé**
**frá** *prep* [*w dat*] from
**fyrir** *prep* [*w acc/dat*] for; over; **ofan fyrir** [*w acc*] down over
**fǫður** *acc/dat/gen of* **faðir**
**gamall** (gǫmul, gamalt; *acc m* gamlan) *adj* old
**hafa** (-ð-) *vb* have; take; **hafa verr** fare worse, get the worst of it
**hallkvæmr** *adj* fit, fitting, effective, advantageous
**hann** (*dat* honum; *pl* þeir) *pron*: *3sg m nom/acc* he, him
**hans** *poss pron*: *sg m* his (*gen of* **hann**)
**heita** (heitir; hét, hétu; heitinn) *vb* be named, be called
**heldr** (*superl* helzt) *comp adj* more, rather
**helzt** *superl adv* most of all, especially (*from* **heldr**)
**herað** *n* district, country
**hestaat** *n* horse-fight
**hestastafr** *m* horse-staff (for use in a horse-fight)
**hestr** *m* horse, stallion
**heyra** (-ð-) *vb* hear, listen to
**hét** *3sg past of* **heita**
**hlaupa** (hleypr; hljóp, hljópu; hlaupinn) *vb* leap, jump; **hlaupa ofan fyrir** fall down over
**hljóp** *3sg past of* **hlaupa**
**Hof** *n* Hof ('Temple') (*place name*)
**hon** *pron*: *3sg f* she
**honum** *pron*: *3sg m dat* (to) him (*see* **hann**)
**hrossamaðr** *m* person who knows horses
**hugr** *m* heart, mind, disposition
**húskarl** *m* man-servant
**hǫgg** *n* stroke, blow
**illa** (*comp* verr) *adv* badly, 'ill'
**í** *prep* [*w dat*] in
**kalla** (-að-) *vb* call
**kalls** *n* mockery, ridicule
**kapítuli** *m* chapter
**kapp** *n* zeal, eagerness, energy
**kenna** (-d-) *vb* know, recognize
**koma** (kemr; kom, kómu; kominn) *vb* come; **koma á** hit
**láta** (lætr; lét, létu; látinn) *vb* let; let on; [*w inf*] have [sb do sth], cause [sb] to [do sth]

**leyna** (-d-) *vb* hide, conceal; **leyna [e-u] [e-n]** hide [sth] from [sb]
**lét** *3sg past of* **láta**
**ljósta** (lýstr; laust, lustu; lostinn) *vb* strike, hit
**maðr** (*gen* manns; *pl gen* manna) *m* man, person, human being
**manna** *gen pl of* **maðr**
**manns** *gen sg of* **maðr**
**margr** (mǫrg, mar(g)t) *adj* [*w sg*] many a (*in collective sense*); [*w pl*] many
**margt** *n adj as indef pron* many a thing (*from* **margr**)
**með** *prep* [*w dat*] with, together with
**meiri** *comp adj* greater; more (*see* **mikill**)
**menn** *pl of* **maðr**
**mikill** (mikil, mikit; *pl* miklir; *comp* meiri) *adj* big, large, great
**mót** *n* meeting; **á móti** in return, in exchange
**munu** (mun, munu; mundi; *pret inf* mundu) *aux vb* will, shall (*futurity*); (*past tense*) would
**mæla** (-t-) *vb* say, speak; appoint, settle; **mæla til** make arrangement for, initiate, be responsible for
**nefna** (-d-) *vb* name, call
**né** *conj* nor
**niðr** *adv* down
**nú** *adv* now
**ofan** *adv* down (from above); **ofan fyrir** [*w acc*] down over
**ok** *conj* and (in addition); *adv* also
**orðit** *n ppart of* **verða**
**ójafnaðarmaðr** *m* unjust man, one who is quarrelsome and overbearing, difficult to deal with
**rann** *3sg past of* **renna**
**rauðavíkingr** *m* 'red' viking, a particularly fierce and violent viking
**rauðr** (rauð, rautt) *adj* red
**reið** *f* act of riding (a horse)
**reiðhestr** *m* riding-horse (*as distinct from a pack-horse*)
**renna** (rennr; rann, runnu; runninn) *vb* run, flee
**rista** (-t-) *vb* cut, scratch
**ríki** *n* realm, kingdom; power
**ríkismaðr** *m* man of power
**sá** (*n* þat; *pl* þeir) *dem pron* that (one)
**sá** *3sg past of* **sjá**
**selja** (-d-) *vb* sell; **selja undan** sell off
**sem** *conj* as; as if
**sér** *refl pron*: *dat* (to) himself (*dat of* **sik**)
**sik** (*dat* sér) *refl pron*: *acc* himself
**sinn** (sín, sitt) *refl poss adj* his, her, its, their (own)
**sinni** *f dat sg of* **sinn**
**síns** *m gen sg of* **sinn**
**sínu** *n dat sg of* **sinn**
**sjá** (sér; sá, sá(u); sénn) *vb* see
**sjálfr** (sjálf, sjálft) *adj* (my-/your-/him-/her-/it-/one-) self
**sjón** *f* sight, eyesight
**sjónlítill** *adj* having poor eyesight
**skoltr** *m* jaw, snout (of an animal)
**skyrta** *f* shirt
**skyrtublað** *n* shirt-lap
**sonr** *m* son
**stangarhǫgg** *n* staff-struck
**stilltr** (stillt, stillt) *adj* calm, even-tempered

**stóðhross** *n* stud-horse
**stǫng** (*gen* stangar) *f* pole, staff
**sunna** *f* sun
**Sunnudalr** *m* Sunnudal (*place name*) ('South Dale', 'South Valley', *or perh* 'Sun Dale')
**svá** *adv* so, thus, such; **svá at (svá ... at)** so that, such that, in such a way that
**til** *prep* [*w gen*] to, for
**um** *prep* [*w acc*] about, in regard to
**undan** *adv* away; **selja undan** sell off
**ungr** (ung, ungt) *adj* young
**upp** *adv* up (*motion*)
**uppaustr** *m* a scooping up
**uppaustrarmaðr** *m* a gossip, babbler (*from* **uppaustr** + **maðr**)
**vann** *3sg past of* **vinna**
**var** *3sg past of* **vera**
**varð** *3sg past of* **verða**
**varðveita** (-tt-) *vb* keep, take care of
**vápn** *n* weapon
**váru** *3pl past of* **vera**
**vel** *adv* well, very
**vera** (er; var, váru; verit) *vb* be
**verða** (verðr; varð, urðu; orðinn) *vb* become; **verða at** become; happen, come about
**verðr** (verð, vert) *adj* worth, worthy, deserving
**verk** *n* work, deed
**verr** *comp adv* worse (*see* **illa**)
**vilja** (vill; vildi; viljat) *vb* wish, want
**vinna** (vinnr; vann, unnu; unninn) *vb* work, perform, labor
**vinr** *m* friend
**vinsæll** (-sæl, -sælt; *comp* -sælli) *adj* popular, blessed with friends
**vinsælli** *comp adj* more popular, better liked (*from* **vinsæll**)
**vist** *f* stay; lodging; **á vist** lodging, staying (at one's house)
**víkingr** *m* viking, sea-raider
**væri** *3sg past subjunct of* **vera**
**þar** *adv* there, at that point
**þat** (*dat* því, *gen* þess) *dem pron*: *sg n nom/acc* that (one) (*see* **sá**)
**þá** *adv* then
**þáttr** *m* short story, tale
**þeim** *pron*: *3pl dat* (to) them (*see* **þeir**)
**þeir** (*dat* þeim) *pron*: *3pl m* they
**þeir** *dem pron*: *pl m* those (*see* **sá**)
**þess** *gen sg of* **þat**
**þessi** (*n* þetta; *dat* þessu) *dem pron*: *sg m/f* this (one)
**þessu** *n dat sg of* **þessi**
**þetta** *n nom/acc sg of* **þessi**
**Þorsteinn** *m* Thorstein (*personal name*)
**Þorvaldr** *m* Thorvald (*personal name*)
**Þórarinn** *m* Thorarin (*personal name*)
**Þórðr** *m* Thord (*personal name*)
**Þórhallr** *m* Thorhall (*personal name*)
**þótt** = **þó at** *conj* [*w subjunct*] although, even though
**þótti** *3sg past of* **þykkja**
**þriggja** *gen of* **þrír**
**þrír** (*gen* þriggja) *num* three
**því** *dat of* **þat**; *as adv* therefore, for that reason; **því at** *conj* because
**þykkja** (þykkir; þótti; þótt) *vb*

*impers* [*w dat*] seem [to sb]
**œpa** (-ð-) *vb* cry out, shout
**œska** *f* youth, childhood
**ǫflugr** (ǫflug, ǫflugt) *adj* strong, powerful
**ǫttu** *3pl past of* **etja**

## 2. KAPÍTULI

Litlu fyrir jól um vetrinn risu konur til verks í Sunnudal. Þá stóð Þorsteinn ok upp ok bar inn hey ok lagðisk síðan niðr í bekk. Nú kemr Þórarinn karl innar, faðir hans, ok spurði, hverr þar lægi. Þorsteinn sagði til sín.

"Hví ertu svá snimma á fótum, sonr?" sagði Þórarinn karl.

Þorsteinn svarar: "Við fá þykki mér at meta þat, sem hér er at vinna,"[35] sagði Þorsteinn.

"Er þér ekki illt í hǫfuðbeinunum,[36] sonr?" kvað Þórarinn karl.

"Eigi kenni ek þess," sagði Þorsteinn.

"Hvat segir þú mér, sonr, af hestaþinginu, því er í fyrra sumar var? Vartu ekki lostinn í svíma, frændi, sem hundr?"

"Engi þykki mér virðing í vera," sagði Þorsteinn, "at kalla þat heldr hǫgg en atburð."[37]

Þórarinn mælti: "Ekki mundi mik þess vara, at ek munda ragan son eiga."[38]

"Mæl þú þat eitt um nú, faðir," sagði Þorsteinn, "er þér þykkir eigi ofmælt síðar."[39]

"Ekki mun ek hér svá mikit um mæla," sagði Þórarinn, "sem

---

[35] **Við fá þykki mér at meta þat, sem hér er at vinna:** 'It seems to me that few (others) are fighting over the work that here needs to be done'.

[36] **Er þér ekki illt í hǫfuðbeinunum:** 'Doesn't your head hurt' (lit., 'is not something ill with you in the headbones').

[37] **Engi þykki mér virðing í vera, ... at kalla þat heldr hǫgg en atburð:** 'I do not think that there is any honor ... in calling it a (deliberate) blow rather than an accident'.

[38] **Ekki mundi mik þess vara, at ek munda ragan son eiga:** 'I would not have expected that I would have a coward for a son'.

[39] **Mæl þú þat eitt um nú, ... er þér þykkir eigi ofmælt síðar:** 'Say about this now only as much (lit., that one [thing]) ... as you will not think overstated later'.

mér er at skapi."[40]

Nú reis Þorsteinn upp ok tók vápn sín ok gekk síðan heiman ok fór, unz hann kom til hrossahúss þess, er Þórðr gætti hesta Bjarna í, ok var hann þar fyrir.

Þá hittir Þorsteinn Þórð ok mælti til hans: "Vita vilda ek þat, Þórðr minn, hvárt þat varð þér váðaverk, er ek fekk af þér hǫgg í fyrra sumar á hestaþingi, eða hefir þat at vilja þínum orðit, [ok hvárt bœta] muntu þá vilja yfir."[41]

Þórðr svarar: "Ef þú átt tvá hváptana, þá bregð þú tungunni sitt sinn í hvárn ok kalla í ǫðrum váðaverk, ef þú vilt, en í ǫðrum kalla þú alvǫru.[42] Ok eru þar nú bœtrnar, þær er þú munt af mér fá."

"Búsk þú þá svá við," sagði Þorsteinn, "at vera má, at ek heimta eigi optar."[43]

Síðan hleypr Þorsteinn at honum ok høggr Þórð banahǫgg, gekk síðan til húss at Hofi ok hitti úti konu eina ok mælti við hana: "Seg þú Bjarna, at naut hafi stangat Þórð,[44] hestasvein hans, ok mun hann bíða þar, til þess er hann kemr, hjá hestahúsinu."

---

[40] **Ekki mun ek hér svá mikit um mæla, ... sem mér er at skapi:** 'I will not speak about it here (at this point) ... as much as I am in the mood (or have a mind) to'.

[41] **eða hefir þat at vilja þínum orðit, ok hvárt bœta muntu þá vilja yfir:** 'or did that happen according to your desire (on purpose), and (if so) will you then be willing to pay compensation'.

[42] **Ef þú átt tvá hváptana, þá bregð þú tungunni sitt sinn í hvárn ok kalla í ǫðrum váðaverk, ef þú vilt, en í ǫðrum kalla þú alvǫru:** 'If you have two cheeks, then stick your tongue into each one in turn and call it in one an accident, if you wish, and in the other call it seriousness (something intentional)'.

[43] **Búsk þú þá svá við, ... at vera má, at ek heimta eigi optar:** 'Be on your guard then, ... for it may be that I will not (come to) collect again'.

[44] **at naut hafi stangat Þórð:** 'that an ox has gored Thord'. Thorstein makes a play on words with his nickname ***stangar****hǫgg* ('staff-struck'). He is the ox who has ***stangat*** ('gored') the man responsible for giving him this derisive nickname. There is similar imagery in *Vápnfirðinga saga,* where the feuding men of the district appear in a prophetic dream as *naut* 'oxen'. In this dream, Bjarni is represented as *rauðr uxi, ok var beinlitr á hornunum, ok var allra nauta skrautligastr* 'a red ox with bone-colored horns, and of all oxen the most splendid', which rose up at Hof and gored (*stangaði*) his father's killer to death.

"Far þú heim, maðr," sagði hon, "en ek segi, þá er mér sýnisk."

Nú ferr Þorsteinn heim, en konan ferr til verks síns.

Bjarni reis upp um morguninn, ok er hann var undir borð kominn, þá spurði Bjarni, hvar Þórðr væri, ok svǫruðu menn, at hann myndi til hrossa farinn.

"Heim hugða ek hann þó mundu kominn," kvað Bjarni, "ef hann væri heill."

Þá tók kona til orða, sú er Þorsteinn hafði hitta:[45] "Satt er þat, er oss er opt sagt konum, at þar er lítit til vits at taka, sem vér erum konur.[46] Hér kom Þorsteinn stangarhǫgg í morgin, kvað naut hafa stangat Þórð, svá at hann myndi eigi sjálfbjargi verða,[47] en ek nennta eigi þá at vekja þik, ok þá hvarf mér ór hug síðan."

Bjarni sté þá undan borði, gekk þá til hrossahússins ok fann þar Þórð veginn, ok var hann síðan jarðaðr.

Bjarni býr nú mál til ok gerir Þorstein sekan um vígit. En Þorsteinn sat heima í Sunnudal ok vann fyrir fǫður sínum, ok lét Bjarni þó kyrrt vera.[48]

## VOCABULARY TO CHAPTER 2

**af** *prep* [*w dat*] of, from; in respect of, concerning; **segja af** tell about

**alvara** *f* seriousness, earnestness, something done in earnest

**annarr** (ǫnnur, annat; *dat m* ǫðrum) *adj* other, another; **annarr ... annarr ...** *indef pron* the one ... the other ...

**at** *inf marker* to

**atburðr** *m* occurrence, accident

**átt** *2sg pres of* **eiga**

**banahǫgg** *n* death-blow

**bani** *m* death

**bar** *vb, see* **bera**

**bein** *n* bone

**bekkr** *m* bench

**bera** (berr; bar, báru; borinn) *vb*

---

[45] **sú er Þorsteinn hafði hitta**, i.e., **hafði (verit at) hitta:** 'the one whom Thorstein had happened to meet'.

[46] **Satt er þat, er oss er opt sagt konum, at þar er lítit til vits at taka, sem vér erum konur:** 'It is true what is often said to us women, that little sense is to be had where we women are (concerned)'.

[47] **svá at hann myndi eigi sjálfbjargi verða:** 'in such a way that he was unable to help himself'.

[48] **lét Bjarni þó kyrrt vera:** 'yet Bjarni let everything lie quiet'.

carry, bear

**bíða** (bíðr; beið, biðu; beðinn) *vb* wait

**borð** *n* table; board, food at table; **koma undir borð** sit at table, come to eat

**bót** (*pl* bœtr) *f* bettering; (*almost always in pl*) atonement, compensation

**bregða** (bregðr; brá, brugðu; brugðinn) *vb* [*w dat*] move quickly; cause to move quickly

**búa** (býr; bjó, bjoggu/bjuggu; búinn) *vb* prepare, make ready; **búa mál til** begin or prepare a lawsuit; *refl* **búask** make oneself ready, equip oneself; **búask við** prepare for, be on one's guard against

**býr** *3sg pres of* **búa**

**bœta** (-tt-) *vb* amend, redress, compensate; **bœta yfir við [e-n]** make good to [sb] for a wrong inflicted

**bœtr** *nom pl of* **bót**

**eða** *conj* or

**ef** *conj* if

**eiga** (á, eigu; átti; áttr) *vb* own, have

**einn** (ein, eitt) *num* one

**eitt** *n of* **einn**

**ek** (*acc* mik, *dat* mér; *pl* vér) *pron*: *1 sg* I

**ekki** *n adj as adv* not (*from* **engi**)

**en** *conj* than; **heldr ... en** rather ... than

**engi** (*n* ekki) *adj/indef pron* no, no one, none

**er** *rel pron/adv* where; which, that; *conj* when; **þá er** when

**ert** *2sg pres of* **vera**

**ertu = ert þú**

**fann** *3sg past of* **finna**

**fara** (ferr; fór, fóru; farinn) *vb* go, travel, move

**farinn** *ppart* (be) gone (*from* **fara**)

**fá** (fær; fekk, fengu; fenginn) *vb* get, take

**fár** (fá, fátt; *pl acc m* fá) *adj* few

**fekk** *3sg past of* **fá**

**ferr** *3sg pres of* **fara**

**finna** (finnr; fann, fundu; fundinn) *vb* find

**fór** *3sg past of* **fara**

**fótr** *m* foot; **vera á fótum** be up, afoot, out of bed

**frændi** *m* kinsman

**fyrir** *adv* before (one), present, at hand

**fyrri** *comp adj* former

**ganga** (gengr; gekk, gengu; genginn) *vb* go, walk

**gera** (-ð-) *vb* make, do, act; (*leg*) set the amount of a fine; **gera [e-n] sekan** condemn [sb] to outlawry

**gæta** (-tt-) *vb* [*w gen*] watch, take care of, hold

**hana** *pron*: *3sg f acc* her (*see* **hon**)

**hann** *pron*: *3sg m* he

**hans** *pron*: *3sg m gen* (of) him (*see* **hann**)

**hefir** *3sg pres of* **hafa**

**heill** (heil, heilt) *adj* healthy, well, 'hale'

**heim** *adv* home, homewards (*motion*)

**heima** *adv* home, at home (*location*)

**heiman** *adv* from home
**heimta** (-t-) *vb* claim (fulfillment of a promise), collect (payment)
**heldr** *comp adj* more, rather; **heldr ... en** rather ... than
**hestahús** *n* stable
**hestasveinn** *m* horse-boy
**hestaþing** *n* meeting for a public horse-fight
**hey** *n* hay
**hér** *adv* here
**hitta** (-tt-) *vb* meet
**hjá** *prep* [*w dat*] by, near
**hlaupa** (hleypr; hljóp, hljópu; hlaupinn) *vb* leap, jump; **hlaupa at [e-m]** attack [sb]
**hon** (*acc* hana) *pron*: *3sg f* she
**hross** *n* horse
**hrossahús** *n* stable
**hugða** *1sg past of* **hyggja**
**hundr** *m* dog
**hús** *n* house, building
**hvar** *int adv* where
**hvarf** *3sg past of* **hverfa**
**hvat** (*dat* hví) *int pron*: *n* what (*see* **hverr**)
**hváptr** *m* cheek
**hvárr** (hvár, hvárt; *acc m* hvárn) *int dual pron* whether, which (of two)
**hvárt** *n int pron as adv/conj* whether (or not) (*from* **hvárr**); **hvárt ... eða** *conj* whether ... or
**hverfa** (hverfr; hvarf, hurfu; horfinn) *vb* be lost, disappear
**hverr** (hver, hvat; *acc m* -jan) *int pron* who
**hví** *int adv* why, for what (*dat of* **hvat**)
**hyggja** (hugð-; hug(a)ðr) *vb* think, believe
**hǫfuð** *n* head
**hǫfuðbein** *n pl* head-bones
**hǫggva** (høggr; hjó, hjoggu/hjuggu; hǫgg(v)inn) *vb* strike, smite
**illr** (ill, illt) *adj* bad, evil, 'ill'
**inn** *adv* in (*motion*)
**innar** *comp adv* farther in (*from* **inn**)
**í** *prep* [*w acc*] in, to, into (*motion*)
**jarða** (-að-) *vb* bury
**jarðaðr** *ppart of* **jarða**
**jól** *n pl* Yule, heathen midwinter festival later applied to Christmas
**karl** *m* man; old man
**kemr** *3sg pres of* **koma**
**koma** (kemr; kom, kómu; kominn) *vb* come
**kominn** *ppart of* **koma**
**kona** *f* woman
**kvað** *3sg past of* **kveða**
**kveða** (kveðr; kvað, kváðu; kveðinn) *vb* say, state, utter
**kyrr** (kyrr, kyrrt) *adj* still, calm, quiet
**lagðisk** *3sg past refl of* **leggja**
**leggja** (lagð-; *ppart* lag(i)ðr~laginn) *vb* lay, place, put; *refl* **leggjask** lay, set oneself
**liggja** (liggr; lá, lágu; leginn) *vb* lie, lie down
**lítill** (lítil, lítit; *dat n* litlu) *adj* little, small; short, brief (*time*); **litlu fyrir** a little before
**lítit** *n adj as indef pron* little (*from* **lítill**)
**ljósta** (lýstr; laust, lustu; lostinn) *vb* strike, hit; **ljósta í svíma**

knock unconscious
**lostinn** *ppart of* **ljósta**
**lægi** *3sg past subjunct of* **liggja**
**má** *3sg pres of* **mega**
**mál** *n* suit, action, case, matter; **búa mál til** prepare or begin a lawsuit
**mega** (má, megu; mátti; mátt) *aux vb* can, may
**meta** (metr; mat, mátu; metinn) *vb* estimate, value; **meta við [= metask um]** dispute over, quarrel about, contend for
**mér** *pron*: *1sg dat* (to) me (*see* **ek**)
**mik** *pron*: *1sg acc* me (*see* **ek**)
**minn** (mín, mitt) *poss adj*: *1sg* my
**morginn** *m* morning; **í morgin** this morning; **um morguninn** in the morning
**morgunn** = **morginn**
**munda** *1sg past of* **munu**
**mundu** *pret inf of* **munu**
**munt** *2sg pres of* **munu**
**muntu** = **munt þú**
**munu** (mun, munu; mundi; *pret inf* mundu) *aux vb* will, shall (*futurity*)
**myndi** *3sg past subjunct of* **munu**
**mæla** (-t-) *vb* say, speak
**naut** *n* ox; cattle, oxen
**nenna** (-t-) *vb* have a desire to, be disposed to
**of** *adv* too, too much
**ofmælt** *n ppart* spoken in excess, overstated (*from* **mæla**)
**opt** (*comp* optar) *adv* often, frequently
**optar** *comp adv* more often (*from* **opt**); **eigi optar** not again
**orð** *n* word; **taka til orða** speak up (**orða** *gen pl*)
**oss** *pron*: *1pl acc/dat* us (*see* **vér**)
**ór** *prep* [*w dat*] out of, from
**ragr** (rǫg, ragt) *adj* cowardly
**rísa** (ríss; reis, risu; risinn) *vb* arise, rise, stand up; **rísa upp** rise up, get up
**sagði** *3sg past of* **segja**
**sagt** *n ppart of* **segja**
**sannr** (sǫnn, satt) *adj* true
**sat** *3sg past of* **sitja**
**satt** *adj, see* **sannr**
**sá** (sú, þat) *dem pron* that (one)
**segja** (sagð-) *vb* say, tell; **segja til sín** give one's name, identify oneself
**sekr** (sek, sekt) *adj* convicted, condemned, outlawed
**sem** *rel pron* which, that (= **er**); *conj* as, like
**sik** (*dat* sér, *gen* sín) *refl pron*: *acc* him-/her-/it-/oneself
**sinn** *n* a time, instance; **sitt sinn** in turn
**sinn** (sín, sitt) *refl poss adj* his, her, its, their (own)
**sitja** (sitr; sat, sátu; setinn) *vb* sit; stay
**sitt** *n acc sg of* **sinn**
**síðan** *adv* then, after that
**síðar** *comp adv* later, afterwards
**sín** *refl pron*: *gen* (of) himself (*see* **sik**)
**sín** *n nom/acc sg of* **sinn**
**sínum** *m dat sg of* **sinn**
**sjálfbjargi** *adj* self-sufficing, self-helpful
**skap** *n* condition of mind, temper, mood
**snimma** *adv* early

**spurði** *3sg past of* **spyrja**
**spyrja** (spurð-) *vb* ask
**standa** (stendr; stóð, stóðu; staðinn) *vb* stand
**stanga** (-að-) *vb* poke, goad; butt, gore (*of cattle*)
**sté** *3sg past of* **stíga**
**stíga** (stígr; steig/sté, stigu; stiginn) *vb* step, tread; **stíga undan borði** get up from the table
**stóð** *3sg past of* **standa**
**sumar** *n* summer
**sú** (*pl* þær) *dem pron*: *sg f* that (one) (*see* **sá**)
**svara** (-að-) *vb* [*w dat*] answer, reply; **svara [e-m] [e-u]** to answer [sth] to [sb]
**svími** *m* swoon; **ljósta í svíma** knock unconscious
**svǫruðu** *3pl past of* **svara**
**sýna** (-d-) *vb* show; *refl* **sýnask** seem, appear; *impers* [*w dat*] seem [to sb]; seem fitting [to sb]
**taka** (tekr; tók, tóku; tekinn) *vb* take, take hold of, grasp; **taka til [e-s]** concern [sth]; **taka til orða** begin to speak, speak up (**orða** *gen pl*)
**til** *prep* [*w gen*] to; until; **til þess er** *conj* until
**tók** *3sg past of* **taka**
**tunga** *f* tongue
**tvá** *acc of* **tveir**
**tveir** (*acc m* tvá) *num* two
**um** *prep* [*w acc*] during, in (*time*)
**undan** *prep* [*w dat*] from under; away from
**undir** *prep* [*w acc*] under, underneath (*motion*)
**unz** *conj* until
**úti** *adv* outside
**vara** (-ð-) *vb impers* [*w gen of thing, acc of person*] expect
**vart** *2sg past of* **vera**
**vartu = vart þú**
**váðaverk** *n* (*leg*) accidental deed, of harm inflicted unintentionally
**vega** (vegr; vá, vágu; veginn) *vb* kill, slay
**vekja** (vakð-) *vb* waken [sb], rouse from sleep
**vera** (er; var, váru; verit) *vb* be
**vetr** (*gen* vetrar) *m* winter; **um vetrinn** in, during the winter
**vér** (*acc/dat* oss) *pron*: *1pl* we (*see* **ek**)
**við** *prep* [*w acc*] with, against
**vilda** *1sg past of* **vilja**
**vilja** (vill; vildi; viljat) *vb* wish, want
**vili** (-j-) *m* will, wish
**virðing** *f* value, worth; honor
**vit** *n* good sense, wit, intelligence
**vita** (veit, vitu; vissi; vitaðr) *vb* know, understand
**víg** *n* killing, (*leg.*) homicide or manslaughter
**yfir** *adv* over
**þá** *adv* then; **þá er** *conj* when
**þér** *pron*: *2sg dat* (to) you (*see* **þú**)
**þik** *pron*: *2sg acc* you (*see* **þú**)
**þinn** (þín, þitt) *poss adj*: *2sg* your
**þó** *adv* yet, nevertheless
**þú** (*acc* þik, *dat* þér) *pron*: *2sg* you
**þykki** *3sg pres subjunct of* **þykkja**
**þykkja** (þykkir; þótti; þótt) *vb impers* [*w dat*] seem [to sb]
**þær** *dem pron*: *pl f* those (*see* **sú**)
**ǫðrum** *m dat sg of* **annarr**

## 3. Kapítuli

Um haustit sátu menn við sviðuelda at Hofi, en Bjarni lá úti á eldahússveggnum[49] ok hlýddi þaðan til tals manna.

Nú taka þeir brœðr til orða, Þórhallr ok Þorvaldr: "Eigi varði oss þess, þegar vér tókum vist með Víga-Bjarna, at vér myndim hér svíða dilkahǫfuð, en Þorsteinn, skógarmaðr hans, skyldi svíða geldingahǫfuð. Væri eigi verra at hafa meir vægt[50] frændum sínum í Bǫðvarsdal ok sæti nú eigi skógarmaðrinn jafnhátt honum í Sunnudal,[51] en lagðir verða forlagðir, ef fyrir sárunum verða,[52] ok eigi vitum vér, hvé nær hann vill þenna flekk má af virðingu sinni."

Maðr einn svaraði: "Slíkt er verr mælt en þagat[53] ok líkligt, at ykkr hafi troll togat tungu ór hǫfði. Ætlum vér, at hann nenni eigi at taka bjǫrg frá fǫður hans sjónlausum ok annarri ómegð þeiri, sem í Sunnudal er. En kynligt þykki mér, ef þit svíðið opt lambahǫfuðin hér eða hrósið því, hvat í Bǫðvarsdal var títt."

Nú fara menn til borða ok síðan til svefns, ok fann ekki á Bjarna,[54] hvat talat hafði verit.

Um morguninn vakði Bjarni þá Þórhall ok Þorvald ok bað þá ríða í Sunnudal ok fœra sér hǫfuð Þorsteins við bolinn skilit at dagmálum, — "ok þykki mér þit," sagði hann, "líkligastir til at

---

[49] **eldahússveggnum**: *veggnum = vegginum*, dat. sg. of *veggr* 'wall' with the suffixed article.

[50] **vægt:** ppart. of *vægja* 'to spare'.

[51] **Væri eigi verra at hafa meir vægt frændum sínum í Bǫðvarsdal ok sæti nú eigi skógarmaðrinn jafnhátt honum í Sunnudal:** 'It would not have been worse (= it would have been better) (for him) to have shown more mercy to his kinsmen in Bodvarsdal, and that this outlaw were not sitting on an equal level with him in Sunnudal'.

[52] **lagðir verða forlagðir, ef fyrir sárunum verða:** *Forlagðir*, meaning 'without (or bereft of) courage', contrasts with *lagðir* 'laid down, placed', also 'stabbed, struck (with a weapon)'. Hence this obscure proverb may mean something like 'those who are struck despair when facing wounds'.

[53] **Slíkt er verr mælt en þagat:** 'Such a thing is worse said than left unsaid'.

[54] **fann ekki á Bjarna:** 'There was no indication that Bjarni took notice'.

fœra flekk af virðingu minni, ef ek hefi ekki þrek til sjálfr."

Nú þykkjask þeir víst ofmælt hafa, ok fara þeir nú þó, unz þeir koma í Sunnudal. Þorsteinn stóð í durum ok hvatti sax.

Ok er þeir kómu þar, þá spurði hann, hvert þeir ætluðu, en þeir sǫgðusk hrossa leita skyldu, en Þorsteinn kvað þeira mundu skammt at leita,[55] — "er hér eru við garð."

"Eigi er víst, at vit finnim hrossin, ef þú vísar okkr eigi gørr til."

Þorsteinn gengr þá út. Ok er þeir koma í garðinn ofan, þá fœrir Þorvaldr upp øxina ok hleypr at honum, en Þorsteinn stakk við honum hendi sinni, svá at hann fell fyrir. Þorsteinn lagði saxinu í gegnum hann. Þá vildi Þórhallr veita honum tilræði, ok hafði hann slíka fǫr sem Þorvaldr.

Þá bindr Þorsteinn á bak báða þá ok lætr upp taumana á háls hestinum ok vísar á leið ǫllu saman,[56] ok ganga hestarnir nú heim til Hofs.

Húskarlar váru úti at Hofi ok gengu inn ok sǫgðu Bjarna, at þeir Þorvaldr váru heim komnir, ok sǫgðu þá eigi ørendlaust farit hafa. Gengr nú Bjarni út ok sér nú, hvernig um er búit, ok hefir ekki orða um fleira,[57] lætr nú jarða þá. Ok er nú kyrrt allt, unz jól líðr.

## VOCABULARY TO CHAPTER 3

**allr** (ǫll, allt; *dat n* ǫllu) *adj* all; *indef pron* everyone; **allt** *n* everything

**bað** *3sg past of* **biðja**

**bak** *n* back

**báðir** (báðar, bæði) *adj/indef dual pron* both

**biðja** (biðr; bað, báðu; beðinn) *vb* ask, request, bid

**bjǫrg** *f* help; provisions, means of subsistence

**bolr** *m* trunk (of a tree, and metaphorically, of a body)

**borð** *n* table; board, food at table;

[55] **þeir sǫgðusk hrossa leita skyldu, en Þorsteinn kvað þeira mundu skammt at leita:** 'they said that they had to search for horses, but Thorstein said that they would not have far to search'.

[56] **Þá bindr Þorsteinn á bak báða þá ok lætr upp taumana á háls hestinum ok vísar á leið ǫllu saman:** 'Then Thorstein binds them both on horseback and sets the reins up on the horses' necks and sends them all together on their way'.

[57] **hefir ekki orða um fleira:** 'he has nothing more to say about it'.

**fara til borða** go to table (**borða** *gen pl*)
**bróðir** (*pl* brœðr) *m* brother
**brœðr** *pl of* **bróðir**
**búa** (býr; bjó, bjoggu/bjuggu; búinn) *vb* prepare
**búit** *n ppart of* **búa**; **búit um** *adv* the state of things
**Bǫðvarsdalr** *m* Bodvarsdal ('Bodvar's Valley') (*place name*)
**dagmál** *n pl* morning meal, breakfast time
**dagr** *m* day
**dilkahǫfuð** *n pl* heads of sucking lambs
**dilkr** *m* sucking lamb
**durum** *dat pl of* **dyrr**
**dyrr** (*pl dat* durum) *n* (*pl*) or *f pl* door
**eldahússveggr** *m* wall of the **eldahús**
**eldahús** *n* 'fire house', main hall of a long house where the fire was kept
**finna** (finnr; fann, fundu; fundinn) *vb* find, find out; **finna á** *impers* let on, give indication that sth is noticed
**fleiri** *comp adj* more (*see* **margr**)
**flekkr** *m* fleck, spot; blot, stain
**forlagðr** *ppart* without or bereft of courage (*from* **leggja**); **verða forlagðr** give up, lose heart, despair
**fœra** (-ð-) *vb* bring, convey; **fœra [e-n] af [e-u]** remove [sth] from [sth]
**fǫr** *f* journey, trip
**garðr** *m* yard, encosure; fence
**gegnum** *adv* through; **í gegnum** *prep* [*w acc*] through
**geldingahǫfuð** *n pl* heads of wethers
**geldingr** *m* wether, gelded sheep
**gørr** *comp adv* more clearly (*from* **gørva**)
**gørva** (*comp* gørr) *adv* quite, clearly
**haust** *n* autumn, fall; **um haustit** in the fall, during the fall
**háls** *m* neck
**hendi** *dat sg of* **hǫnd**
**hlaupa** (hleypr; hljóp, hljópu; hlaupinn) *vb* leap, jump
**hleypr** *3sg pres of* **hlaupa**
**hlýða** (-dd-) *vb* [*w dat*] listen; **hlýða til** listen to
**hrósa** (-að-) *vb* [*w dat*] boast (of), gloat (over); praise
**hvat** *rel pron* what, that which
**hvatti** *3sg past of* **hvetja**
**hvernig** *int adv* how, in what way
**hvert** *adv* to where (*motion*), whither
**hvetja** (hvatt-) *vb* whet, sharpen
**hvé** *int adv* how; to what extent; **hvé nær** when
**hǫnd** (*dat* hendi) *f* hand
**illr** (ill, illt) *adj* bad, evil, 'ill'
**jafnhár** (-hár, -hátt) *adj* as high
**jafnhátt** *n adj as adv* equally, evenly, as high (*from* **jafnhár**)
**koma** (kemr; kom, kómu; kominn) *vb* come
**kómu** *3pl past of* **koma**
**kynligr** (-lig, -ligt) *adj* strange, wonderful, extraordinary
**lagðr** *ppart of* **leggja**
**lamb** *n* lamb
**lambahǫfuð** *n pl* lambs' heads

**lá** *3sg past of* **liggja**
**láta** (lætr; lét, létu; látinn) *vb* put, place, set
**lagði** *3sg past of* **leggja**
**leggja** (lagð-; *ppart* lag(i)ðr~laginn) *vb* lay, place, put; [*w dat*] stab, thrust
**leið** *f* road, way; **á leið** on the way
**leita** (-að-) *vb* [*w gen*] seek, search for
**líða** (líðr; leið, liðu; liðinn) *vb* pass (by)
**líkligr** (-lig, -ligt; *superl* líkligastr) *adj* likely, probable
**lætr** *3sg pres of* **láta**
**margr** (mǫrg, mar(g)t; *comp* fleiri) *adj* many
**má** (mái; máði; máðr) *vb* blot out, efface
**mál** *n* meal, mealtime
**meir** *comp adv* more (*see* **mjǫk**)
**mjǫk** *adv* much
**munu** (mun, munu; mundi; *pret inf* mundu) *aux vb* will, shall (*futurity*)
**myndim** *1pl past subjunct of* **munu**
**nær** *conj* when; **hvé nær** when
**okkr** *pron*: *1dual acc/dat* us (two) (*see* **vit**)
**ómegð** *f* the state of being dependent; (*coll*) those who are unable to support themselves
**ríða** (ríðr; reið, riðu; riðinn) *vb* ride, go on horseback
**saman** *adv* together
**sax** *n* short sword
**sár** *n* wound
**sátu** *3sg past of* **sitja**
**segja** (sagð-) *vb* say, tell
**sér** *refl pron*: *dat* (to) him-/her-/it-/oneself, themselves (*see* **sik**)
**sik** (*dat* sér, *gen* sín) *refl pron*: *acc* him-/her-/it-/oneself
**sitja** (sitr; sat, sátu; setinn) *vb* sit; stay
**sjónlauss** (-laus, -laust) *adj* blind
**skammr** (skǫmm, skammt) *adj* short, brief
**skammt** *n adj as adv* a short distance, not far (*from* **skammr**)
**skilit** *n ppart of* **skilja**
**skilja** (-d/ð-, *ppart* skiliðr~skildr~skilinn) *vb* part, separate, divide; **skiliðr við** parted from, separated from
**skógarmaðr** *m* outlaw, 'woodsman'
**skógr** (*gen* -ar) *m* forest, woods
**skulu** (skal, skulu; skyldi; *pret inf* skyldu) *aux vb* shall (*obligation, purpose, necessity, fate*); (*past tense*) should
**skyldi** *3sg past of* **skulu**
**skyldu** *pret inf of* **skulu**
**slíkr** (slík, slíkt) *adj* such; like; **slíkr sem** such as, similar to
**stakk** *3sg past of* **stinga**
**stinga** (stingr; stakk, stungu; stunginn) *vb* thrust, stick, stab; **stinga hendi við [e-m]** shove [sb] with the hand or arm
**svefn** *m* sleep; **fara til svefns** go to sleep
**sviðueldr** *m* fire for roasting sheep's heads
**svíða** (svíðr; sveið, sviðu; sviðinn) *vb* burn, singe
**sæti** *3sg past subjunct of* **sitja**
**sǫgðu** *3pl past of* **segja**

**sǫgðusk** *3pl past refl of* **segja**
**taka** (tekr; tók, tóku; tekinn) *vb* take; **taka [e-t] frá [e-m]** take [sth] from [sb], deprive [sb] of [sth]
**tal** *n* talk, conversation
**tala** (-að-) *vb* talk, speak
**taumr** *m* rein
**tilræði** *n* assault (with a weapon); **veita [e-m] tilræði** make an assault on [sb]
**tíðr** (tíð, títt) *adj* frequent; usual; often spoken of; **hvat var títt** what had happened
**toga** (-að-) *vb* draw, tug, pull
**tókum** *1pl past of* **taka**
**troll** *n* troll
**út** *adv* out (*motion*)
**vakði** *3sg past of* **vekja**
**veggr** *m* wall
**veita** (-tt-) *vb* grant, give; help, assist; allow, permit; **veita [e-m] tilræði** make an assault on [sb]
**vekja** (vakð-) *vb* waken [sb], rouse from sleep
**verða** (verðr; varð, urðu; orðinn) *vb* become; happen; **verða fyrir [e-u]** meet with [sth]
**verri** *compar adj* worse (*see* **illr**)
**við** *prep* [*w acc*] by, close to
**vilja** (vill; vildi; viljat) *vb* wish, want
**virðing** *f* reputation, honor
**vit** (*acc/dat* okkr) *pron*: *1dual* we (two) (*see* **ek**)
**vísa** (-að-) *vb* show, point out, indicate; **vísa [e-m] til [e-s]** show, point out [to sb] [sth]; **vísa [e-m] á leið** point [sb] on the way
**víss** (vís, víst) *adj* certain; wise
**víst** *n adj as adv* certainly, for sure (*from* **víss**)
**vægja** (-ð-) *vb* [*w dat*] spare
**ykkr** *pron*: *2dual acc/dat* you (two) (*see* **þit**)
**þaðan** *adv* from there
**þagat** *n ppart of* **þegja**
**þá** *pron*: *3pl m acc* them (*see* **þeir**)
**þegar** *conj* as soon as
**þegja** (þagð-, *ppart* þagat) *vb* be silent; be quiet
**þeir** (*acc* þá) *pron*: *3pl m* they
**þenna** *m acc sg of* **þessi**
**þessi** (*acc* þenna) *dem pron*: *sg m/f* this (one)
**þit** (*acc/dat* ykkr) *pron*: *2dual* you (two) (*see* **þú**)
**þrek** *n* strength, courage, fortitude; **hafa þrek til [e-s]** have the courage to do [sth]
**þykkjask** *refl vb* consider oneself
**ætla** (-að-) *vb* think, expect, suppose; intend, purpose, mean
**ǫllu** *dat sg n of* **allr**
**ørendlaust** *adv* without purpose, in vain, for nothing; **fara ørendlaust** go in vain
**øx** *f* ax

## 4. KAPÍTULI

Þá tekr Rannveig til orða einn aptan, er þau kómu í sæng sína,

Bjarni ok hon: "Hvat ætlar þú, at nú sé tíðast talat í heraðinu?" kvað hon.

"Eigi veit ek," sagði Bjarni. "Margir þykki mér ómerkir í sínum orðum," sagði hann.

"Þat er nú tíðast at rœða, at menn þykkjask eigi vita, hvat Þorsteinn stangarhǫgg mun þess gera, at þér muni þurfa þykkja at hefna.[58] Hefir hann nú vegit húskarla þína þrjá. Þykkir þingmǫnnum þínum eigi vænt til halds, þar sem þú ert, ef þessa er óhefnt, ok eru þér mjǫk mislagðar hendr í kné."[59]

Bjarni svarar: "Nú kemr hér at því, sem mælt er, at engi lætr sér annars víti at varnaði,[60] en hlýða mun ek þér, hvat er þú mælir. Hefir Þorsteinn ok fá saklausa drepit."

Hætta þau þessu tali ok sofa af um nóttina.

Um morguninn vaknar Rannveig, er Bjarni tók ofan skjǫld sinn, ok spurði hon, hvert hann skyldi.

Hann svarar: "Nú skal skipta virðingu með okkr Þorsteini[61] í Sunnudal," segir hann.

"Hversu fjǫlmennr skaltu fara?" segir hon.

"Ekki mun ek draga fjǫlmenni at Þorsteini," segir hann, "ok mun ek einn fara."

"Gerðu eigi þat," segir hon, "at hætta þér einn undir vápn

---

58 **Þat er nú tíðast at rœða, at menn þykkjast eigi vita, hvat Þorsteinn stangarhǫgg mun þess gera, at þér muni þurfa þykkja at hefna:** 'What is now most widely gossiped about is that people cannot imagine what Thorstein Staff-Struck will have to do before you think it necessary to seek redress'.

59 **Þykkir þingmǫnnum þínum eigi vænt til halds, þar sem þú ert, ef þessa er óhefnt, ok eru þér mjǫk mislagðar hendr í kné:** 'Your thingmen (supporters) do not consider there to be much hope of support where you are concerned, if this remains unavenged, for your hands are very much mislaid on your knees'. Rannveig is accusing Bjarni of doing nothing (he keeps his hands in his lap) when he should act.

60 **Nú kemr hér at því, sem mælt er, at engi lætr sér annars víti at varnaði:** 'Now it comes to this point, just as the saying goes, that no one takes another's punishment as warning'.

61 **Nú skal skipta virðingu með okkr Þorsteini í Sunnudal:** 'Now Thorstein and I will put honor to the test', lit., 'honor will be exchanged between us', meaning that their reputations will be settled by fighting.

heljarmannsins."

Bjarni mælti: "Mun þér nú eigi verða þeira kvenna dœmi,[62] er þat gráta á annarri stundu, er eggja á annarri? En ek þoli opt lengi frýjuorð bæði þér ok ǫðrum, en þá stoðar ok ekki at letja mik, þá er ek vil fara."[63]

## Vocabulary to Chapter 4

**aptann** *m* evening
**báðir** (báðar, bæði) *adj/indef dual pron* both
**bæði** *n adj as adv* both (*from* **báðir**); **bæði ... ok** *conj* both ... and
**draga** (dregr; dró, drógu; dreginn) *vb* drag, draw, pull
**drepa** (drepr; drap, drápu; drepinn) *vb* kill, slay
**dœmi** *n* example
**eggja** (-að-) *vb* egg on, incite, goad
**einn** (ein, eitt) *adj* (*following the noun it modifies*) alone, only
**eru** *3sg pres of* **vera**
**fjǫlmenni** *n* many people, a crowd
**fjǫlmennr** (-menn, -mennt) *adj* with many people; **hversu fjǫlmennr** with how many men
**frýja** *f* taunt, challenge, reproach
**frýjuorð** *n* taunt, accusation of cowardice
**ger** *2sg imp of* **gera**
**gera** (-ð-) *vb* do
**gerðu = ger þú**
**gráta** (grætr; grét, grétu; grátinn) *vb* cry, weep; [*w acc*] bewail, weep for
**hald** *n* support, backing
**hefna** (-d-) *vb* [*w gen*] avenge, take vengeance
**Hel** (-j-) *f* hell, the abode of the dead; death; *also* Hel, goddess of death (*mythological name*)
**heljarmaðr** *m* powerful, rough man, 'man of Hel'
**hendr** *pl of* **hǫnd**
**hversu** *adv* how; **hversu fjǫlmennr** with how many men
**hætta** (-tt-) *vb* [*w dat*] leave off, cease; *impers* risk, venture
**hǫnd** (*pl* hendr) *f* hand
**kné** *n* knee
**lengi** *adv* long, for a long time; **opt lengi** too long
**letja** (latt-) *vb* hold back, deter, dissuade

---

[62] **Mun þér nú eigi verða þeira kvenna dœmi:** 'Will you not now become like (lit., an example of) one of those women'.

[63] **ek þoli opt lengi frýjuorð bæði þér ok ǫðrum, en þá stoðar ok ekki at letja mik, þá er ek vil fara:** 'I have too long endured accusations/taunts of cowardice both from you and others, and it is no use trying to deter me when I am determined to go'.

**maðr** (*pl* menn) *m* man, person, human being

**mislagðr** *ppart* mislaid (*from* **misleggja**); **[e-m] eru mislagðar hendr í kné** one has 'mislaid hands' upon the knees, does not act when one should

**misleggja** (-lagð-; *ppart* -lag(i)ðr) *vb* lay amiss

**muni** *3sg pres subjunct of* **munu**

**munu** (mun, munu; mundi; *pret inf* mundu) *aux vb* will, shall (*futurity*)

**nótt** *f* night; **um nóttina** through the night

**óhefndr** *ppart* unavenged (*from* **hefna**)

**ómerkr** (ómerk, ómerkt) *adj* insignificant, silly

**Rannveig** *f* Rannveig (*personal name*)

**rœða** (-dd-) *vb* speak, chat, gossip

**saklauss** (-laus, -laust) *adj* innocent

**sé** *3sg pres subjunct of* **vera**

**sinn** (sín, sitt) *refl poss adj* his, her, its, their (own)

**sína** *f acc sg of* **sinn**

**sínum** *dat pl of* **sinn**

**skal** *3sg pres of* **skulu**

**skalt** *2sg pres of* **skulu**

**skaltu** = **skalt þú**

**skipta** (-t-) *vb* [*w dat*] divide, share, deal out; **skipta með [e-m]** exchange with [sb]

**skjǫldr** *m* shield

**skulu** (skal, skulu; skyldi; *pret inf* skyldu) *aux vb* shall (*obligation, purpose, necessity, fate*)

**sofa** (sefr; svaf, sváfu; sofinn) *vb* sleep; **sofa af (um nóttina)** sleep through the night

**stoða** (-að-) *vb* avail, be of use

**stund** *f* a while, a certain length of time; **á annarri stundu ... á annarri** at one time ... at another, now ... then

**sæng** *f* bed

**taka** (tekr; tók, tóku; tekinn) *vb* take

**tala** (-að-) *vb* talk, speak

**tekr** *3sg pres of* **taka**

**tíðast** *n adj as adv* most commonly; most widely spoken (*from* **tíðastr**)

**tíðastr** *superl adj* most common; most widely spoken of (*from* **tíðr**)

**tíðr** (tíð, títt) *adj* frequent; usual; often spoken of

**vakna** (-að-) *vb* awaken, wake up

**varnaðr** *m* warning, caution

**vega** (vegr; vá, vágu; veginn) *vb* kill, slay

**vera** (er; var, váru; verit) *vb* be

**vilja** (vill; vildi; viljat) *vb* wish, want

**víti** *n* fine, punishment

**vænn** (væn, vænt) *adj* promising, likely, to be expected; **þykkir [e-m] eigi vænt til [e-s]** [sb] is not confident of [sth]

**þar** *adv* there; **þar sem** *conj* where

**þat** (*dat* því) *dem pron*: *sg n* that

**þau** *pron*: *3pl n nom/acc* they, them (*n, mixed*)

**þessa** *n gen sg of* **þessi**

**þessi** (*gen n* þessa) *dem pron*: *sg m/f* this (one)

**þing** *n* assembly
**þingmaðr** *m* liegeman of a particular chieftain
**þinn** (þín, þitt) *poss adj*: *2sg* your, yours (*sg*)
**þína** *m acc pl of* **þinn**
**þínum** *dat pl of* **þinn**
**þola** (-ð-; *ppart* þol(a)t) *vb* suffer, endure, bear; **þola [e-t] [e-m]** endure [sth] from [sb]
**þrír** (*acc* þrjá) *num* three
**þrjá** *acc of* **þrír**
**þurfa** (þarf, þurfu; þurfti; þurft) *vb* need
**því** *dat of* **þat**; **hér at því** to this point
**ǫðrum** *dat pl of* **annarr**

## 5. KAPÍTULI

Bjarni ferr nú í Sunnudal, ok stendr Þorsteinn í durum, ok kǫstuðusk þeir á nokkurum orðum.

Bjarni mælti: "Þú skalt til einvígis[64] ganga við mik í dag, Þorsteinn, á hól þenna, er hér er túni."[65]

"Allt er mér til þess vant," kvað Þorsteinn, "at berjask við þik,[66] en ek skal þegar útan, er skip ganga, því at ek kann drengskap þinn, at þú munt fá fǫður mínum forverk, ef ek fer frá."

"Ekki stoðar nú undan at mælask,"[67] segir Bjarni.

"Leyfa muntu mér þá, at ek finna fǫður minn áðr?" sagði Þorsteinn.

"At vísu," sagði Bjarni.

Þorsteinn gekk inn ok sagði fǫður sínum, at Bjarni var þar kominn ok bauð honum til einvígis.

---

[64] *Einvigi* and *hólmganga* were two types of single combat. The rules for *einvígi* were straightforward; the rules for *hólmganga* were strict and complicated. Olaf Bø, "Hólmganga and Einvígi: Scandinavian Forms of the Duel," in *Mediaeval Scandinavia,* 1969, pp. 132-148; Marlene Ciklamini, "The Old Icelandic Duel," in *Scandinavian Studies,* 1963, pp. 175-194; Jesse Byock, "Hólmganga," in *Medieval Scandinavia: An Encyclopedia,* eds. Pulsiano & Wolf 1993, p. 289.

[65] **túni = í túni**.

[66] **Allt er mér til þess vant ... at berjask við þik:** 'I have absolutely no desire to fight with you'.

[67] **Ekki stoðar nú undan at mælask:** 'There is no use now trying to talk your way out from under this'.

Þorarinn karl svaraði: "Ván má hverr maðr þess vita, ef hann á við sér ríkara mann ok siti samheraðs honum ok hafi þó gǫrt honum nǫkkura ósœmð, at hann mun eigi mǫrgum skyrtum slíta, ok kann ek því ekki at sýta þik, at mér þykkir þú mikit til hafa gǫrt.[68] Tak nú vápn þín ok ver þik sem skǫruligast, því at þar mundi verit hafa minnar ævi, at ekki munda ek bograt hafa fyrir slíkum, sem Bjarni er.[69] Er Bjarni þó inn mesta kappi. Þykki mér ok betra at missa þín en eiga ragan son."

Nú gengr Þorsteinn út, ok fara þeir síðan út á hólinn ok taka til at berjask með harðfengi, ok hjuggusk mjǫk hlífar fyrir hvárum tveggja.

Ok þá er þeir hǫfðu mjǫk lengi barizk, þá mælti Bjarni til Þorsteins: "Þyrstir mik nú, því at ek em óvanari erfiðinu en þú."

"Gakk þú þá til lœkjarins," sagði Þorsteinn, "ok drekk."

Bjarni gerði svá ok lagði niðr sverðit hjá sér.

Þorsteinn tók upp, leit á ok mælti: "Eigi mundir þú þetta sverð hafa í Bǫðvarsdal."

Bjarni svaraði engu.

Ganga þeir nú upp á hólinn ok berjask um stundar sakar, ok þykkir Bjarna maðrinn vígkœnn ok þykkir fastligra fyrir en hann hugði.[70]

"Margt hendir mik nú í dag," sagði Bjarni. "Lauss er nú skóþvengr minn."

---

68 **Ván má hverr maðr þess vita, ef hann á við sér ríkara mann ok siti samheraðs honum ok hafi þó gǫrt honum nǫkkura ósœmð, at hann mun eigi mǫrgum skyrtum slíta, ok kann ek því ekki at sýta þik, at mér þykkir þú mikit til hafa gǫrt:** 'Every man can be sure of this expectation, if he has dealings with a more powerful man and dwells in the same district with him, and yet has done him some dishonor, that he will not (live long enough to) wear out many shirts; and I cannot mourn for you (when you die), because to me it seems that you have done a great deed'.

69 **því at þar mundi verit hafa minnar ævi, at ekki munda ek bograt hafa fyrir slíkum, sem Bjarni er:** 'because in my time, I would not have bowed before such men as Bjarni'.

70 **þykkir Bjarna maðrinn vígkœnn ok þykkir fastligra fyrir en hann hugði:** 'Bjarni considers the man to be skillful in fighting and more steadfast than he had thought'.

"Bind þú hann þá," kvað Þorsteinn.

Nú lýtr Bjarni niðr, en Þorsteinn gekk inn ok hefir út skjǫldu tvá ok sverð eitt, gengr nú á hólinn til Bjarna ok mælti við hann: "Hér er skjǫldr ok sverð, er faðir minn sendi þér, ok mun þetta eigi sljóvgask meir í hǫggunum en þat, sem þú hefir áðr. Nenni ek ok eigi at standa hlífarlauss lengr undir hǫggum þínum, en gjarna vilda ek nú hætta þessum leik, því at ek em hræddr, at meira muni mega gæfa þín en ógipta mín, ok er hverr frekr til fjǫrsins um alla þraut, ef ek mætta nǫkkuru um ráða."[71]

"Eigi mun nú stoða at beiðask undan," sagði Bjarni, "berjask skal enn."[72]

"Eigi munda ek frekt hǫggva," sagði Þorsteinn.

Þá høggr Bjarni allan skjǫldin af Þorsteini, en þá hjó Þorsteinn skjǫldinn af Bjarna.

"Stórt er nú hǫggvit," kvað Bjarni.

Þorsteinn svaraði: "Ekki hjóttu smæra hǫgg."

Bjarni mælti: "Betr bítr þér nú it sama vápnit, er þú hefir áðr í dag haft."

Þorsteinn mælti: "Spara munda ek við mik óhapp, ef ek mætta svá gera, ok berjumk ek hræddr við þik. Vilda ek enn allt á þínu valdi vera láta."[73]

Þá átti Bjarni at hǫggva,[74] ok var nú hvárrtveggi hlífarlauss. Bjarni mælti þá: "Þat mun illt kaup at taka glœp við miklu happi.[75] Ætla ek mér fullgoldit fyrir þrjá húskarla mína þik einn,[76] ef þú

---

[71] **at meira muni mega gæfa þín en ógipta mín, ok er hverr frekr til fjǫrsins um alla þraut, ef ek mætta nǫkkuru um ráða:** 'that your good luck will avail more than my bad luck, and every man is eager for life in every struggle, if I might somehow decide on this'.

[72] **mun ... skal**, impersonal.

[73] **Vilda ek enn allt á þínu valdi vera láta:** 'I would still be willing to let you decide in everything' (lit., 'let everything be in your power').

[74] **átti Bjarni at hǫggva:** 'it was Bjarni's turn'.

[75] **Þat mun illt kaup at taka glœp við miklu happi:** 'It would be a bad bargain to take a misdeed over great luck'.

[76] **þik einn:** 'you alone', acc. obj. of *ætla*. The sentence is equal to: *Ek ætla þik einn (hafa) mér fullgoldit fyrir þrjá húskarla mína* 'I consider you alone to have fully paid me for my three household servants'. The sense is that

vilt mér trúr vera."

Þorsteinn sagði: "Orðit hafa mér svá fœri í dag á þér, at ek mætta svíkja þik, ef ógæfa mín gengi ríkara en lukka þín, ok mun ek eigi svíkja þik,"[77] sagði Þorsteinn.

"Sé ek, at þú ert afbragðsmaðr," sagði Bjarni. "Lofa muntu mér, at ek ganga inn til fǫður þíns," sagði hann, "ok segja honum slíkt, sem ek vil?"

"Gakk, sem þú vilt, fyrir mínum sǫkum," kvað Þorsteinn, "ok far þó varliga."

## VOCABULARY TO CHAPTER 5

**afbragðsmaðr** *m* outstanding man, a man of great ability
**allr** (ǫll, allt) *adj* all
**allt** *n adj as adv* all, entirely, altogether (*from* **allr**)
**á** *3sg pres of* **eiga**
**áðr** *adv* before; first
**barizk** *n ppart of* **berjask**
**bauð** *3sg past of* **bjóða**
**beiða** (-dd-) *vb* ask, request, beg; *refl* **beiðask** request on one's own behalf; **beiðask undan** excuse oneself, beg off
**berja** (barð-) *vb* beat, strike; *refl* **berjask** fight
**berjumk** *1sg pres of* **berjask**
**betr** *comp adv* better (*see* **vel**)
**betri** *comp adj* better (*see* **góðr**)
**bjóða** (býðr; bauð, buðu; boðinn) *vb* [*w dat*] bid, order, enjoin
**bogra** (-að-) *vb* creep along bowed or stooping; **bogra fyrir [e-m]** bow before [sb]
**dagr** *m* day; **í dag** today
**drekka** (drekkr; drakk, drukku; drukkinn) *vb* drink
**drengskapr** *m* courage, valor; noble-mindedness, integrity
**eiga** (á, eigu; átti; áttr) *vb* own, have; have to, be obligated to, have a right to, be entitled to; **eiga við [e-n]** have to do with [sb], deal with [sb]
**einvígi** *n* single combat
**ekki** (*dat* engu) *n indef pron* nothing (*from* **engi**)
**em** *1sg pres of* **vera**
**engi** (*n* ekki; *dat* engu) *indef pron* no, no one, none
**engu** *dat of* **ekki**

---

Bjarni considers Thorstein alone to be full payment for his three slain servants.

[77] **Orðit hafa mér svá fœri í dag á þér, at ek mætta svíkja þik, ef ógæfa mín gengi ríkara en lukka þín, ok mun ek eigi svíkja þik:** 'I have had enough chance at you today that I might have betrayed you, if my ill fortune had proved more powerful than your luck, and I will not betray you'.

**erfiði** *n* toil, labor, hard work; trouble; distress, suffering
**fara** (ferr; fór, fóru; farinn) *vb* go, travel, move
**fastligr** (-lig, -ligt; *comp* -ligastr) *adj* firm, strong
**fer** *1sg pres of* **fara**
**fjǫr** *n* life
**forverk** *n* humble work, farm work
**frá** *adv* away
**frekr** (frek, frekt) *adj* greedy, eager
**frekt** *n adj as adv* greedily, eagerly (*from* **frekr**)
**fullgoldit** *n ppart* fully paid (*from* **gjalda**)
**fyrir** *adv* before, ahead, above
**fœri** *n* means, occasion, opportunity
**gakk** *2sg imp of* **ganga**
**ganga** (gengr; gekk, gengu; genginn) *vb* go, walk
**ganga** *1sg pres subjunct of* **ganga**
**gekk** *3sg past of* **ganga**
**gengi** *3sg past subjunct of* **ganga**
**gengr** *3sg pres of* **ganga**
**gera** (-ð-) *vb* make, do, act; **gera til [e-s]** earn [sth]
**gjalda** (geldr; galt, guldu; goldinn) *vb* pay; repay, return
**gjarna** *adv* willingly, gladly; rather
**glœpr** *m* crime, misdeed
**góðr** (góð, gott; *comp* betri) *adj* good
**gæfa** *f* luck
**gǫrt** = **gert** *n ppart of* **gera**
**hafa** (-ð-) *vb* have; take
**hafi** *3sg pres subjunct of* **hafa**
**haft** *n ppart of* **hafa**
**happ** *n* good luck (*with the notion of happenstance*)
**harðfengi** *f* hardihood, valor, vigor
**henda** (-d-) *vb* catch; **[e-n] hendir [e-t]** [sb] is caught in, overtaken by [sth] (as a fault, ill luck, etc.), [sth] befalls [sb]
**hjó** *3sg past of* **hǫggva**
**hjótt** *2sg past of* **hǫggva**
**hjóttu** = **hjótt þú**
**hjuggusk** *3pl past of* **hǫggvask**
**hlíf** (*pl* -ar) *f* cover, protection (*esp* of a shield or armor)
**hlífarlauss** (-laus, -laust) *adj* uncovered, unprotected, without shield or armor
**hóll** *m* hill, hillock
**hræddr** (hrædd, hrætt) *adj* afraid, frightened; **hræddr við [e-n/e-t]** afraid of [sb/sth]
**hugði** *3sg past of* **hyggja**
**hvárrtveggi** = **hvárrtveggja**
**hvárrtveggja** *indef dual pron* each (of two); both
**hvárum tveggja** *dat of* **hvárrtveggja**
**hverr** (hver, hvat; *acc m* -jan) *adj/indef pron* each, every; everyone
**hyggja** (hugð-; hug(a)ðr) *vb* think, believe
**hǫfðu** *3pl past of* **hafa**
**høggr** *3sg pres of* **hǫggva**
**hǫggva** (høggr; hjó, hjoggu/hjuggu; hǫgg(v)inn) *vb* strike, smite; *refl* **hǫggvask** exchange blows, fight; **hǫggvask fyrir** hack away
**kann** *3sg pres of* **kunnu**

**kappi** *m* hero, champion
**kasta** (-að-) *vb* [*w dat*] throw, cast; *refl* **kastask** cast against one another; **kastask á orðum** exchange words
**kaup** *n* bargain, trade
**kunna** (kann, kunnu; kunni; kunnat) *vb* know; be able to
**kǫstuðusk** *3pl past refl of* **kasta**
**lauss** (laus, laust) *adj* loose, free, unimpeded
**leikr** (*dat* leik) *m* game, play, sport
**leit** *3sg past of* **líta**
**lengr** *comp adv* longer
**leyfa** (-ð-) *vb* permit, allow
**líta** (lítr; leit, litu; litinn) *vb* look, see, behold; **líta á** look at
**lofa** (-að-) *vb* allow, permit
**lukka** *f* luck
**lúta** (lýtr; laut, lutu; lotinn) *vb* bow down, bend down
**lýtr** *3sg pres of* **lúta**
**lœkr** (*gen* -jar) *m* brook, rivulet
**maðr** (*acc* mann) *m* man, person, human being
**mann** *acc sg of* **maðr**
**margr** (mǫrg, mar(g)t) *adj* many
**mega** (má, megu; mátti; mátt) *vb* be able, have strength to accomplish, avail
**meira** *n of* **meiri**
**meiri** *comp adj* greater; more (*see* **mikill**)
**mestr** *superl adj* greatest, biggest; 'most' (*see* **mikill**)
**mikill** (mikil, mikit; *superl* mestr) *adj* big, large, great
**mikit** *n adj as adv* greatly, much
**minn** (mín, mitt) *poss adj*: *1sg* my
**missa** (-t-) *vb* [*w gen*] lose, miss, lack
**mín** *f gen sg of* **minn**
**mína** *m acc pl of* **mína**
**mínum** *m dat sg and dat pl of* **mína**
**munu** (mun, munu; mundi; *pret inf* mundu) *aux vb* will, shall (*futurity*)
**mælask** *refl vb* speak, express oneself; **mælask undan** excuse oneself, talk one's way out
**mætta** *1sg past subjunct of* **mega**
**mǫrgum** *dat pl* **margr**
**nǫkkurr** (nǫkkur, nǫkkut) *adj/ indef pron* one, some, a certain
**nǫkkuru** *adv* somehow, in any way (*n dat sg of* **nǫkkurr**)
**ógipta** *f* ill-luck, haplessness
**ógæfa** *f* ill-luck
**óhapp** *n* ill-luck, mishap
**ósœmð** *f* disgrace, dishonor
**óvanari** *comp adj* less accustomed (*from* **vanr**)
**ráða** (ræðr; réð, réðu; ráðinn) *vb* advise; decide, have one's way; **ef ek má ráða** if I can have it as I like
**ríkari** *comp adj* stronger, more powerful (*from* **ríkr**)
**ríkr** (rík, ríkt; *comp* ríkari) *adj* strong, powerful
**sakar** *nom/acc pl of* **sǫk**
**samheraðs** *adv* within the same district
**samr** (sǫm, samt) *adj* same
**senda** (-d-) *vb* send
**sé** *1sg pres of* **sjá**
**siti** *3sg pres subjunct of* **sitja**
**sitja** (sitr; sat, sátu; setinn) *vb* sit;

stay
**sjá** (sér; sá, sá(u); sénn) *vb* see
**skal** *1sg pres of* **skulu**
**skip** *n* ship
**skjǫldr** *m* shield
**skjǫldu** *acc pl of* **skjǫldr**
**skór** *m* shoe
**skóþvengr** *m* 'shoe-thong', shoe-string
**skulu** (skal, skulu; skyldi; *pret inf* skyldu) *aux vb* shall (*obligation, purpose, necessity, fate*)
**skyrta** *f* shirt
**skǫruligast** *n adj as adv* bravely, boldly (*from superl of* **skǫru-ligr**); **sem skǫruligast** as bravely as possible
**skǫruligr** (-lig, -ligt; *superl* skǫru-ligastr) *adj* brave, bold, manly
**slíta** (slítr; sleit, slitu; slitinn) *vb* [*w dat*] rend, tear; wear out (*of clothes*)
**sljóvgask** *refl vb* grow slow, dull, blunt (*of a sword*)
**smár** (smá, smátt; *comp* smæri) *adj* small, little
**smæri** *comp adj* smaller (*from* **smár**)
**spara** (-ð-; *ppart* spar(a)ðr) *vb* spare; **spara [e-t] við sik** spare oneself from, shrink from [sth]
**standa** (stendr; stóð, stóðu; staðinn) *vb* stand
**stendr** *3sg pres of* **standa**
**stórr** (stór, stórt) *adj* big, great; powerful
**stund** (*gen* -ar) *f* a while, a certain length of time; **um stundar sakar** for a while
**sverð** *n* sword
**svíkja** (svíkr; sveik, sviku; svikinn) *vb* betray
**sýta** (-t-) *vb* wail, lament, mourn for
**sǫk** (*gen* sakar; *pl* sakar/sakir) *f* cause, reason, 'sake'; **fyrir mínum sǫkum** for my part; **um stundar sakar** for a while
**taka** (tekr; tók, tóku; tekinn) *vb* take; **taka til at** [*w inf*] begin to [do sth]
**trúr** (trú, trútt) *adj* faithful, true, loyal
**tún** *n* home-field, i.e., the enclosed field in front of a homestead; also, a farmhouse and its buildings
**undir** *prep* [*w dat*] under, underneath (*location*)
**útan** *adv* abroad, away from Iceland (usu. denoting Norway)
**vald** *n* power, might, authority
**vandr** (vǫnd, vant) *adj* hard, difficult; **allt vandr** altogether difficult
**vanr** (vǫn, vant; *comp* vanari) *adj* accustomed, usual, wont; **vera vanr [e-u]** be accustomed to [sth]
**vant** *n of* **vandr**
**varliga** *adv* warily, carefully
**ván** *f* hope, expectation
**vel** *adv* well, very
**ver** *2sg imp of* **verja**
**vera** (er; var, váru; verit) *vb* be
**verja** (varð-, var(i)ðr) *vb* defend
**vilja** (vill; vildi; viljat) *vb* wish, want
**víg** *n* fight, battle
**vígkœnn** (-kœn, -kœnt) *adj* skill-ful in fighting, 'battle-keen'

**víss** (vís, víst) *adj* certain; **at vísu** certainly, of course
**þegar** *adv* immediately; **þegar er** as soon as
**þessi** (*dat m* þessum) *dem pron*: *sg m/f* this (one)
**þessum** *dat sg of* **þessi**
**þinn** (þín, þitt) *poss adj*: *2sg* your (*sg*)
**þín** *pron*: *2sg gen* of you (*see* **þú**)
**þín** *n nom/acc pl of* **þinn**
**þíns** *m gen sg of* **þinn**
**þínu** *n dat sg of* **þinn**
**þraut** *f* struggle, great exertion
**þú** (*acc* þik, *dat* þér, *gen* þín) *pron*: *2sg* you
**þvengr** *m* thong
**þyrsta** (-t-) *vb impers* [*w acc*] be thirsty; **þyrstir mik** I am thirsty
**ævi** (*gen* ævi) *f* age, time

## 6. KAPÍTULI

Þá gekk Bjarni at lokhvílu þeiri, er Þórarinn karl lá í. Þórarinn spurði þá, hverr þar fœri, en Bjarni sagði til sín.

"Hvat segir þú tíðenda,[78] Bjarni minn?" kvað Þórarinn.

"Víg Þorsteins, sonar þíns," kvað Bjarni.

"Varðisk hann nǫkkut?" kvað Þórarinn.

"Engan mann ætla ek snarligra verit hafa í vápnskipti en Þorstein, son þinn."

"Eigi er kynligt at því," kvað karl, "at þungt veitti við þik í Bǫðvarsdal, er þú bart nú af syni mínum"[79]

Þá mælti Bjarni: "Ek vil bjóða þér til Hofs, ok skaltu sitja þar í ǫðru ǫndvegi, meðan þú lifir, ok mun ek vera þér í sonar stað."

"Svá er mér farit," kvað karl, "sem þeim, er ekki eigu undir sér, ok verðr heitum heimskr maðr feginn.[80] En svá eru heit yður hǫfðingja, þá er þér vilið fróa manninn eptir slíka atburði, at þat

[78] **Hvat segir þú tíðenda:** 'What news do you have', lit., 'what do you say of news (tidings)?'

[79] **Eigi er kynligt at því, ... at þungt veitti við þik í Bǫðvarsdal, er þú bart nú af syni mínum:** 'It is not strange to believe ... that it must have been hard to deal with you in Bodvarsdal, since you have now defeated my son'.

[80] **Svá er mér farit, ... sem þeim, er ekki eigu undir sér, ok verðr heitum heimskr maðr feginn:** 'It has turned out for me ... the same as for those who have control over nothing, and (only) a foolish man takes delight in promises'.

er mánaðarfró, en þá erum vér virðir eptir þat sem aðrir framfœrslumenn, ok fyrnask við þat seint várir harmar.[81] En sá maðr, er handsǫl tekr af slíkum manni, sem þú ert, má þó vel una sínum hlut, hvat sem at dœma er.[82] Mun ek ok þessi handsǫl taka af þér, ok gakk þú nú hingat til mín í rekkjugólfit, ok verðr þú nær at ganga, því at karl skelfr nú allr á fótum fyrir elli sakar ok vanheilsu, en eigi trútt, at mér hafi eigi í skap runnit sonardauðinn."[83]

Bjarni gekk nú í rekkjugólfit ok tók í hǫnd Þórarni karli. Hann fann þá, at hann þuklaði á saxi ok vildi þá leggja at Bjarna.

Hann kippði hendinni ok mælti: "Allra fretkarla armastr!" sagði Bjarni. "Nú mun at makligleika fara með okkr.[84] Þorsteinn, sonr þinn, lifir, ok skal hann fara heim með mér til Hofs, en þér skal fá þræla til forverks, ok skal þér einskis vant, meðan þú lifir."

Þorsteinn fór nú heim með Bjarna til Hofs ok fylgði honum allt til dauðadags ok þótti nær einskis manns maki vera at drengskap ok hreysti.

Bjarni helt vel virðingu sinni ok var hann því vinsælli ok betr stilltr sem hann var ellri ok var allra manna þrautbeztr ok gerðisk trúmaðr mikill inn síðasta hluta ævi sinnar. Bjarni fór útan ok gekk suðr ok andaðisk í þeiri ferð. Hann hvílir í borg þeiri, er Vateri heitir, ok er þat mikil borg, skammt hingat frá Rómaborg.[85]

---

[81] **þá er þér vilið fróa manninn eptir slíka atburði, at þat er mánaðarfró, en þá erum vér virðir eptir þat sem aðrir framfœrslumenn, ok fyrnask við þat seint várir harmar:** 'when you desire to relieve a man after such events, but that turns out to be only a month's rest, and then our worth is set the same as other paupers', and our sorrows are forgotten but slowly'.

[82] **sá maðr, er handsǫl tekr af slíkum manni, sem þú ert, má þó vel una sínum hlut, hvat sem at dœma er:** 'the man who shakes hands in bargain with a man such as you can nonetheless be content with his lot, whatever the outcome is'.

[83] **eigi trútt, at mér hafi eigi í skap runnit sonardauðinn:** 'it is not likely that I am not affected by the death of my son'.

[84] **Nú mun at makligleika fara með okkr:** 'Now our affairs shall proceed according to what you deserve', lit., 'now it will proceed with us as (things) deserved'.

[85] Another manuscript, AM 162 C fol., has [*sót*]*ti heim inn sæla Petrum* ('visited the home of the blessed Peter') in place of *gekk suðr* ('went south').

Bjarni varð kynsæll maðr. Hans sonr var Skegg-Broddi, er víða kemr við sǫgur ok var inn mesti afbragðsmaðr um sína daga. Dóttir Bjarna hét Halla, móðir Guðríðar, er Kolbeinn lǫgsǫgumaðr átti. Yngvildr var ok dóttir Bjarna, er Þorsteinn Síðu-Hallsson átti, ok var þeira sonr Magnús, faðir Einars, fǫður Magnúss byskups. Ámundi var ok sonr Þorsteins ok Yngvildar. Hann átti Sigríði, dóttur Þorgríms blinda. Hallfríðr var ok dóttir Ámunda, [móðir Ámunda], fǫður Guðmundar, fǫður Magnúss goða ok Þóru, er Þorvaldr Gizurarson átti, ok annarrar Þóru, móður Orms Svínfellings. Guðrún var ok Ámunda dóttir, móðir Þórdísar, móður Helgu, móður Guðnýjar Bǫðvarsdóttur, móður Sturlusona, Þórðar ok Sighvats ok Snorra. Rannveig var ok Ámunda dóttir, móðir Steins, fǫður Guðrúnar, móður Arnfríðar, er Digr-Helgi átti. Þorkatla var ok Ámunda dóttir, [móðir] Arnbjargar, móður Finns prests ok Þorgeirs ok Þuríðar. Ok hefir margt hǫfðingsmanna frá þeim komit.

Ok lýkr þar at segja frá Þorsteini stangarhǫgg.

## VOCABULARY TO CHAPTER 6

**aðrir** *m pl of* **annarr**
**anda** (-að-) *vb* breathe; *refl* **andask** die, breathe one's last
**annarr** (ǫnnur, annat; *dat n* ǫðru; *pl m* aðrir) *adj/indef pron* other; *ord* second, the next following
**armr** (ǫrm, armt; *superl* armastr) *adj* wretched, wicked (*used in swearing*)
**at** *prep* [*w acc*] after
**atburði** *acc pl of* **atburðr**
**atburðr** *m* occurrence, incident, event
**bart** *2sg past of* **bera**
**bera** (berr; bar, báru; borinn) *vb* carry, bear; **bera af** excel, surpass
**bjóða** (býðr; bauð, buðu; boðinn) *vb* [*w dat*] invite
**blindr** (blind, blint) *adj* blind
**borg** *f* fortified town, city
**byskup** *m* bishop
**dauðadagr** *m* day of death
**dauði** *m* death
**dóttir** (*acc/dat/gen* dóttur) *f* daughter
**dœma** (-d/ð-) *vb* give judgement, pass sentence
**eiga** (á, eigu; átti; áttr) *vb* own, have; **eiga undir sér** have in one's power, under one's control
**einskis** *gen sg of* **engi** *and* **ekki**
**ek** (*gen* mín) *pron: 1sg* I
**ekki** (*gen* einskis) *n indef pron* nothing (*from* **engi**)
**elli** *f* old age; **fyrir elli sakar**

because of old age

**ellri** *comp adj* older, elder (*see* **gamall**)

**engan** *acc sg of* **engi**

**engi** (*n* ekki; *acc m* engan, *gen* einskis) *indef pron* no, no one, none

**eptir** *prep* [*w acc*] after

**erum** *1pl pres of* **vera**

**fara** (ferr; fór, fóru; farinn) *vb* go; turn out

**feginn** (-in, -it) *adj* glad, happy, pleased; **verða feginn [e-u]** rejoice in [sth]

**ferð** (-ir) *f* journey, trip

**fótr** *m* foot; **á fótum** on one's feet

**framfœrsla** *f* support, maintenance

**framfœrslumaðr** *m* pauper

**frá** *prep* [*w dat*] from, about; **segja frá [e-u]** tell about [sth]

**fretkarl** *m* 'fart-churl', scoundrel

**fretr** *m* fart

**fró** *f* relief, comfort

**fróa** (-að-) *vb* relieve

**fylgja** (-ð-) *vb* [*w dat*] follow; back, help, side with, support

**fyrnask** (-ð-) *refl vb* grow old, decay; be forgotten

**fœri** *3sg past subjunct of* **fara**

**gamall** (gǫmul, gamalt; *acc m* gamlan; *comp* ellri/eldri) *adj* old

**gerask** *refl vb* become, grow to be

**goði** *m* chieftain-priest

**gólf** *n* chamber, closet, compartment

**halda** (heldr; hélt, héldu; haldinn) *vb* [*w dat*] keep, retain, preserve

**handsal** (handsǫl) *n* (*usu pl*) (*leg*) handshake deal, bargain, transference of a right or duty to another by joining hands

**harmr** *m* grief, sorrow

**heilsa** *f* health

**heimskr** *adj* foolish, silly

**heit** *n* solemn promise, vow

**hingat** *adv* to here (*motion*), hither

**hluti** *m* part

**hlutr** (*dat* hlut) *m* share, part; thing; condition, lot

**hreysti** *f* valour, prowess

**hvíla** *f* bed

**hvíla** (-ð/d-) *vb* rest, lie, sleep

**hǫfðingi** (-j-) *m* chieftain, leader; captain

**hǫfðingsmaðr** *m* man of noble extraction or character; generous person

**kippa** (-t/ð-) *vb* [*w dat*] pull, snatch

**koma** (kemr; kom, kómu; kominn) *vb* come; **koma við [e-t]** touch [sth]; **koma við sǫgur** appear in sagas

**kynsæll** (-sæl, -sælt) *adj* blessed with good and great offspring

**leggja** (lagð-; *ppart* lag(i)ðr~laginn) *vb* lay, place, put; [*w dat*] stab, thrust; **leggja at** attack

**lifa** (-ð-; *ppart* lifat) *vb* live

**lok** *n* bolt, lock

**lokhvíla** *f* locked bed-closet

**lúka** (lýkr; lauk, luku; lokinn) *vb* [*w dat*] close; end, conclude

**lǫg** *n pl* law, laws

**lǫgsǫgumaðr** *m* law-speaker

**maðr** (*dat* manni) *m* man, person

**maki** *m* match

**makligleikr** *m* (*usu pl*) that which

one deserves, serves one right; **at makligleik(a)** deservedly, according to one's just deserts

**makligr** (-lig, -ligt) *adj* fitting, proper, deserving

**manni** *dat sg of* **maðr**

**mánaðarfró** *f* a month's rest

**mánaðr** (*gen* -ar) *m* month

**meðan** *conj* while, as long as

**mín** *pron*: *1sg gen* of me (*see* **ek**)

**móðir** (*acc/dat/gen* móður) *f* mother

**nær** *adv* near; nearly

**nǫkkurr** (nǫkkur, nǫkkut) *indef adj* some, a certain

**nǫkkut** *n adj as adv* somewhat (*from* **nǫkkurr**)

**prestr** *m* priest

**rekkja** *f* bed

**rekkjugólf** *n* a bed-closet

**renna** (rennr; rann, runnu; runninn) *vb* run; **[e-t] rennr [e-m] í skap** *impers* [sb] takes [sth] to heart, is much affected by [sth]

**Rómaborg** *f* the city of Rome (*place name*)

**runnit** *n ppart of* **renna**

**saga** *f* story, saga

**sal** (*pl* sǫl) *n* bargain, sale

**segja** (sagð-) *vb* say, tell; **segja frá [e-u]** tell about [sth]

**seinn** (sein, seint) *adj* slow

**seint** *n adj as adv* slowly, at a slow pace (*from* **seinn**)

**síðastr** *superl adj* last

**síðr** (síð, sítt) *adj* long, hanging

**skap** *n* condition of mind, temper, mood; **[e-t] rennr [e-m] í skap** *impers* [sb] takes [sth] to heart, is much affected by [sth]

**skegg** *n* beard

**Skegg-Broddi** *m* Beard-Broddi (*personal name*)

**skelfr** *3sg pres of* **skjálfa**

**skjálfa** (skelfr; skalf, skulfu; skolfinn) *vb* shiver, shake, quiver

**snarligr** (-lig, -ligt; *comp* -ligri) *adj* keen, quick

**sonar** *gen sg of* **sonr**

**sonardauðr** *m* death of a son

**sonr** (*gen* -ar, *pl* synir) *m* son

**staðr** *m* place, stead; **í [e-s] stað** in place of [sb/sth]

**stilltr** (stillt, stillt) *adj* calm, even-tempered

**suðr** *adv* southwards

**sú** (*dat* þeiri) *dem pron*: *sg f* that (one)

**syni** *acc pl of* **sonr**

**sǫgur** *nom/acc pl of* **saga**

**taka** (tekr; tók, tóku; tekinn) *vb* take, take hold of, grasp; **taka í hǫnd** take by the hand

**tíðendi** *n pl* news, tidings

**trúmaðr** *m* true believer, good Christian

**trúr** (trú, trútt) *adj* faithful, true, loyal; believing; safe; **eigi trútt, at...** it is not likely that...

**trútt** *n of* **trúr**

**una** (-ð/d-) *vb* [*w dat*] love; be content with, enjoy

**van-** *pref* under-, un-, prefix denoting lack

**vanheilsa** *f* poor health, illness

**vanr** (vǫn, vant) *adj* [*w gen*] lacking, wanting; **einskis vanr** lacking nothing

**varðisk** *3sg past refl of* **verja**

**Vateri** *m* Vateri (*place name*)

**vápnskipti** *n* exchange of weapons; exchange of blows

**várr** (vár, várt) *poss adj*: *1pl* our

**veita** (-tt-) *vb* grant, give; **veitti þungt við [e-n]** it proved difficult to deal with [sb]

**verða** (verðr; varð, urðu; orðinn) *vb* become; happen; [*w inf*] must (*necessity*); **verðr þú nær at ganga** you must come near

**verja** (varð-, var(i)ðr) *vb* defend; *refl* **verjask** defend oneself

**virða** (-ð-) *vb* consider, value, estimate the worth of

**virðr** *ppart of* **virða**

**víða** *adv* widely, far and wide, in many places

**yðarr** (yður, yðart; *pl n* yður) *poss adj*: *2pl* your

**yður** *n nom/acc pl of* **yðarr**

**þeira** *poss pron*: *3pl* their

**þeiri** *dat sg of* **sú**

**þessi** (*pl n* þessi) *dem pron*: *sg m/f* this (one)

**þér** (*acc/dat* yðr, *gen* yðar) *pron*: *2 pl* you

**þrautbeztr** *superl adj* best in struggles, most persevering (*see* **þrautgóðr**)

**þrautgóðr** (-góð, -gott) *adj* persevering, steadfast in difficulties

**þræll** *m* bondservant, slave, thrall

**þukla** (-að-) *vb* grope, feel, touch; **þukla á [e-u]** grope for [sth]

**þungr** (þung, þungt) *adj* heavy; oppressive; weighty

**því** *dat of* **þat**; *as adv* [*w comp*] the (more); **því vinsælli** the better liked, the more popular

**ǫðru** *n dat sg of* **annarr**

**ǫndvegi** *n* high-seat, seat of honor; **sitja í ǫðru ǫndvegi** sit in the second high-seat, the next-highest seat of honor

## Vocabulary
## to *Þorsteins þáttr stangarhǫggs*

### Order of the Alphabet

The alphabetical order of the vocabulary is: **a, á, b, d/ð, e, é, f, g, h, i, í, j, k, l, m, n, o, ó, p, r, s, t, u, ú, v, y, ý, x, z, þ, æ, œ, ǫ/ø.** Long vowels with accent are listed after the corresponding short vowels without accent (**a**, then **á**). At the end of the alphabet, **æ** and **œ** are listed separately while **ǫ** and **ø** are listed together.

### Notes on the Vocabulary

**Strong Nouns.** The principal declension classes are indicated by the following conventions:

**Masculine.** The genitive singular and nominative plural endings are given. For example, **hestr** (-s; -ar) *m* horse. **vinr** (-ar; -ir) *m* friend.

**Feminine.** The nominative plural ending is given. For example, **ferð** (-ir) *f* journey, trip; **reið** (-ar) *f* ride, the act of riding.

**Neuter.** The nominative/accusative plural is shown when there is vowel alternation. For example, **sal** (sǫl) *n* bargain, sale.

**Adjectives.** The strong feminine and neuter nominative singular forms are provided. For example, **allr** (ǫll, allt) *adj* all; **feginn** (-in, -it) *adj* glad, happy, pleased; **kyrr** (kyrr, kyrrt) *adj* still, calm, quiet; **stórr** (stór, stórt) *adj* big, great. In addition, the strong masculine accusative singular is given where necessary to indicate a stem-final *-j-* or *-v-*. For example, **ríkr** (rík, ríkt; *acc m* -jan) *adj* powerful; **hár** (há, hátt; *acc m* hávan) *adj* high, tall.

**Strong Verbs.** The principal parts are given: 3sg pres; 3sg past, 3pl past; past participle. For example, **fara** (ferr; fór, fóru; farinn) *vb* go, travel.

**Weak Verbs.** The notation *-að-* indicates a weak verb with the vocalic link *-a-*. For example, **kalla** (-að-) *vb* call (past *kall**aði*** 'called'). For weak verbs without vocalic link, the dental suffix

alone is given (*-t-*, *-d-*, or *-ð-*). For example, **mæla** (-t-) *vb* speak (past *mæl**t**i* 'spoke'). When a past tense dental is added to a verb whose stem already ends in a dental, the two dentals often assimilate. In such instances, the vocabulary indicates the outcome. For example, **beiða** (-dd-) *vb* ask, request; **hitta** (-tt-) *vb* meet; **senda** (-d-) *vb* send (past *bei**dd**i* 'requested', *hi**tt**i* 'met', *sen**d**i* 'sent'). Where the past-tense stem differs from that of the present, the vocabulary provides the full stem. For example, **spyrja** (spurð-) *vb* ask (past ***spurð**i* 'asked').
**PRETERITE-PRESENT VERBS:** The principal parts are given: 3sg pres, 3pl pres; 3sg past; past participle. For example, **eiga** (á, eigu; átti; áttr) *pret-pres vb* own, have, possess; **vita** (veit, vitu; vissi; vitaðr) *pret-pres vb* know, understand.

**PHRASES AND IDIOMS:** Verbs and prepositions take their objects in various cases, depending on sometimes unpredictable usage. This vocabulary adopts the Icelandic convention of using the pronoun *einnhverr/eitthvat* 'somebody/something' to indicate the object cases used in particular phrases. The notation is also useful for distinguishing whether the object is a person or thing.

**[e-n]** (einhvern) = [sb] (somebody), accusative
**[e-t]** (eitthvat) = [sth] (something), accusative
**[e-m]** (einhverjum) = (for) [sb], dative
**[e-u]** (einhverju) = (for) [sth], dative
**[e-s]** (einhvers) = (of) [sb] or [sth], genitive

Examples:
**fœra [e-n] af [e-u]** remove [sth] from [sth]
**taka [e-t] frá [e-m]** take [sth] from [sb], deprive [sb] of [sth]
**þykkir [e-m] eigi vænt til [e-s]** [sb] is not confident of [sth]

## ABBREVIATIONS

| | | | |
|---|---|---|---|
| *1dual, 2dual* | 1st person dual, etc. | *acc* | accusative |
| *1pl, 2pl, 3pl* | 1st person plural, etc. | *adj* | adjective |
| *1sg, 2sg, 3sg* | 1st person singular, etc. | *adv* | adverb |
| | | *art* | article (*def*) |

| | |
|---|---|
| *aux* | auxiliary (*vb*) |
| *coll* | collectively |
| *comp* | comparative (*adj* or *adv*) |
| *conj* | conjunction |
| *dat* | dative |
| *def* | definite (*art*) |
| *dem* | demonstrative (*pron*) |
| *e-m* | *einhverjum* 'for somebody' (*dat*) |
| *e-n* | *einhvern* 'somebody' (*acc*) |
| *e-s* | *einhvers* 'of somebody/something' (*gen*) |
| *e-t* | *eitthvat* 'something' (*acc*) |
| *e-u* | *einhverju* 'for something' (*dat*) |
| *esp* | especially |
| *etc* | et cetera |
| *f* | feminine |
| *gen* | genitive |
| *imp* | imperative |
| *impers* | impersonal (*vb*) |
| *indecl* | indeclinable |
| *indef* | indefinite (*pron*) |
| *inf* | infinitive |
| *interrog* | interrogative (*adv* or *pron*) |
| *leg* | legal usage |
| *lit* | literally |
| *m* | masculine |
| *n* | neuter |
| *neg* | negative |
| *nom* | nominative |
| *num* | number |
| *obj* | object |
| *ord* | ordinal (*num*) |
| *perh* | perhaps |
| *pers* | personal |
| *pl* | plural |
| *poss* | possessive (*pron*) |
| *ppart* | past participle |
| *pref* | prefix |
| *prep* | preposition |
| *pres* | present |
| *pret-pres* | preterite-present (*vb*) |
| *pron* | pronoun |
| *refl* | reflexive (*vb* or *pron*) |
| *rel* | relative (*pron*) |
| *sb* | somebody |
| *sg* | singular |
| *sth* | something |
| *str* | strong (*adj* or *vb*) |
| *subjunct* | subjunctive |
| *superl* | superlative (*adj* or *adv*) |
| *trans* | transitive (*vb*) |
| *transl* | translation |
| *usu* | usually |
| *vb* | verb |
| *w* | with |
| *wk* | weak (*adj* or *vb*) |
| = | equals |
| ~ | alternative form |

**aðrir** *m pl of* **annarr**

**af** *prep* [*w dat*] off (of); of, from; in respect of, concerning; **segja af** tell about; **sofa af (um nóttina)**

sleep through the night

**afbragðsmaðr** (*acc* -mann, *dat* -manni, *gen* -manns; *pl* -menn, etc.) *m* great man

**allr** (ǫll, allt) *adj* all; *indef pron* all, everyone; **allt** *n* everything

**allt** *n adj as adv* all, entirely, altogether (*from* **allr**)

**alvara** *f* seriousness, earnestness, something done in earnest

**anda** (-að-) *vb* breathe; *refl* **andask** die, breathe one's last

**annarr** (ǫnnur, annat; *acc m* annan, *f* aðra, *dat m* ǫðrum, *n* ǫðru; *pl m* aðrir, *dat* ǫðrum) *adj/indef pron* other, another; *ord* second, the next following; **annarr ... annarr ...** *indef pron* the one ... the other ...

**aptann** <*dat* aptni, *gen* aptans, *pl* aptnar> *m* evening

**armr** (ǫrm, armt; *superl* armastr) *adj* wretched, wicked (*used in swearing*)

**at** *prep* [*w acc*] after; [*w dat*] at, in; as to, with respect to; on account of, by reason of

**at** *conj* that; so that; **því at** because

**at** *inf marker* to

**at** *n* incited conflict or fight (*from* **etja**)

**atburðr** (-ar; -ir) *m* occurrence, incident, event; accident

**auga** *n* eye

## Á

**á** *prep* [*w acc*] on, onto (*motion*); [*w dat*] on, in, at (*location or time*)

**á, átt, átti** *vb, see* **eiga**

**áðr** *adv* before; first

## B

**bað** *vb, see* **biðja**

**bak** (bǫk) *n* back

**banahǫgg** *n* death-blow

**bani** *m* death

**bar, bart** *vb, see* **bera**

**barizk** *ppart, see* **berjask**

**bauð** *vb, see* **bjóða**

**báðir** (báðar, bæði; *gen* beggja) *adj/indef dual pron* both

**beiða** (-dd-) *vb* ask, request, beg; *refl* **beiðask** request on one's own behalf; **beiðask undan** excuse oneself, beg off

**bein** *n* bone

**beinlitr** *m* bone-colored

**bekkr** (*dat* bekk, *gen* -jar; *pl* -ir, *dat* -jum, *gen* -ja) *m* bench

**bera** (berr; bar, báru; borinn) *vb* carry, bear; **bera af** excel, surpass

**berja** (barð-) *vb* beat, strike; *refl* **berjask** fight

**berjumk** *vb, see* **berjask**

**betr** *comp adv* better (*see* **vel**)

**betri** *comp adj* better (*see* **góðr**)

**biðja** (biðr; bað, báðu; beðinn) *vb* ask, request, bid

**binda** (bindr; batt, bundu; bundinn) *vb* bind, tie

**bíða** (bíðr; beið, biðu; beðinn) *vb* wait, 'bide'

**bíta** (bítr; beit, bitu; bitinn) *vb* bite; *refl* **bítask** bite each other, fight (*of horses*)

**Bjarni** *m* Bjarni (*personal name*)

**bjó** *vb, see* **búa**

**bjóða** (býðr; bauð, buðu; boðinn) *vb* [*w dat*] bid, order, enjoin; invite

**bjǫrg** (*gen* bjargar; *pl* bjargir) *f* help; provisions, means of subsistence

**blað** (blǫð) *n* leaf; skirt of a shirt or cloak

**blindr** (blind, blint) *adj* blind

**bogra** (-að-) *vb* creep along bowed or stooping; **bogra fyrir [e-m]** bow before [sb]

**bolr** (-s; -ar) *m* trunk (of a tree, and metaphorically, of a body)

**borð** *n* table; board, food at table; **fara til borða** go to table; **koma undir borð** sit at table, come to eat; **stíga undan borði** get up from the table

**borg** (-ir) *f* fortified town, city

**bót** (bœtr) *f* bettering; (*almost always in pl*) atonement, compensation

**bregða** (bregðr; brá, brugðu; brugðinn) *vb* [*w dat*] move quickly; cause to move quickly; break off, leave off; give up; *refl* **bregðask** fail, fall short, disappoint

**bróðir** (*acc/dat/gen* bróður; *pl* brœðr, *dat* brœðrum, *gen* brœðra) *m* brother

**brún** (brýnn) *f* eyebrow

**brœðr** *m, see* **bróðir**

**bú** *n* home, house; farm, farmstead

**búa** (býr; bjó, bjoggu/bjuggu; búinn) *vb* live (in a place), dwell; prepare, make ready; **búa mál til** prepare or begin a lawsuit; **búa um [e-n]** attend to, take care of [sth]; *refl* **búask** make oneself ready, equip oneself; **búask við** prepare for, be on one's guard against

**búit** *ppart, see* **búa**; **búit um** *adv* the state of things

**byskup** (-s; -ar) *m* bishop

**býr** *vb, see* **búa**

**bæði** *n adj as adv* both (*from* **báðir**); **bæði ... ok** *conj* both ... and

**bœta** (-tt-) *vb* amend, redress, compensate; **bœta yfir við [e-n]** make good to [sb] for a wrong inflicted

**bœtr** *f, see* **bót**

**Bǫðvarsdalr** (*dat* -dal, *gen* -dals) *m* Bodvarsdal ('Bodvar's Valley') (*place name*)

# D

**dagmál** *n pl* morning meal, breakfast time

**dagr** (*dat* degi, *gen* dags; *pl* dagar) *m* day; **í dag** today

**dalr** (*dat* dal, *gen* -s; *pl* -ar~ir) *m* valley, dale

**dauðadagr** (*dat* -degi, *gen* -dags; *pl* -dagar) *m* day of death

**dauði** *m* death

**dilkahǫfuð** *n pl* heads of sucking lambs

**dilkr** *m* sucking lamb

**dóttir** (*acc/dat/gen* dóttur; *pl* dœtr, *dat* dœtrum, *gen* dœtra) *f* daughter

**draga** (dregr; dró, drógu; dreginn) *vb* drag, draw, pull

**drekka** (drekkr; drakk, drukku; drukkinn) *vb* drink

**drengskapr** (*gen* -ar) *m* courage, valor; noble-mindedness, honesty, integrity

**drepa** (drepr; drap, drápu; drepinn) *vb* kill, slay

**durum** *n, see* **dyrr**

**dyrr** (*pl dat* durum, *gen* dura) *n* (*pl*) or *f pl* door

**dæld** *f* gentleness

**dældarmaðr** (*acc* -mann, *dat* -manni, *gen* -manns; *pl* -menn, etc.) *m* gentle, easy man

**dœma** (-d/ð-) *vb* give judgement, pass sentence

**dœmi** *n* example

# E

**eða** *conj* or

**ef** *conj* if

**eggja** (-að-) *vb* egg on, incite, goad

**eiga** (á, eigu; átti; áttr) *vb* own, have, possess; be related to; have to, be obligated to, have a right to, be entitled to; **eiga undir sér** have in one's power, under one's control; **eiga við [e-n]** have to do with [sb], deal with [sb]

**eigi** *adv* not

**einn** (ein, eitt) *num* one; *adj* a, an, a certain one; (*following the noun it modifies*) alone, only

**einskis** *gen sg of* **engi** *and* **ekki**

**einvígi** *n* single combat

**eitt** *num, see* **einn**

**ek** (*acc* mik, *dat* mér, *gen* mín; *dual* vit; *pl* vér) *pron*: *1sg* I

**ekki** (*gen* einskis) *indef pron*: *n* nothing (*see* **engi**)

**ekki** *n adj as adv* not

**eldahús** (*also* eldhús) *n* 'fire house', main hall of a long house where the fire was kept

**eldahússveggr** (-ar~s; -ir) *m* wall of the **eldahús**

**eldaskáli** *m* 'firehall' = **eldahús**

**elli** *f* old age; **fyrir elli sakar** because of old age

**ellri** (*also* eldri) *comp adj* older, elder (*see* **gamall**)

**em** *vb, see* **vera**

**en** *conj* but; and (on the other hand); than (*in comparisons*); **heldr ... en** rather ... than

**engi** (engi, ekki; *acc m* engan, *gen* einskis; *pl* engir) *adj/indef pron* no, no one, none

**engu** *indef pron, see* **ekki**

**enn** *adv* yet, still

**eptir** *prep* [*w acc*] after

**er** *rel pron/adv* where; who, which, that; *conj* when; **þá er** when

**er, ert, eru, erum** *vb, see* **vera**

**erfiði** *n* toil, labor, hard work; trouble; distress, suffering

**ertu = ert þú**

**etja** (etr; atti, ǫttu; attr) *vb* [*w dat*] incite, egg on to fight

# F

**faðir** (*acc* fǫður, *dat* fǫður~feðr, *gen* fǫður; *pl* feðr, *dat* feðrum, *gen* feðra) *m* father

**falla** (fellr; fell, fellu; fallinn) *vb* fall; **falla niðr** be dropped, forgotten

**fann** *vb, see* **finna**

**fara** (ferr; fór, fóru; farinn) *vb* go, travel, move; turn out

**farinn** *ppart* (be) gone (*from* **fara**)

**fastligr** (-lig, -ligt; *comp* -ligastr) *adj* firm, strong

**fá** (fær; fekk, fengu; fenginn) *vb* get, take

**fár** (fá, fátt; *acc m* fán, *f* fá, *dat m* fám, *n* fá; *pl f* fár; *comp* fær(r)i, *superl* fæstr) *adj* few

**feðgar** *m pl* father and son(s)

**feginn** (-in, -it) *adj* glad, happy, pleased; **verða feginn [e-u]** rejoice in [sth]

**fekk** *vb, see* **fá**

**fell** *vb, see* **falla**

**fer** *vb, see* **fara**

**ferð** (-ir) *f* journey, trip

**ferr** *3sg pres of* **fara**

**fé** (*dat* fé, *gen* fjár; *pl dat* fjám, *gen* fjá) *n* property; money, wealth

**félítill** (-lítil, -lítit; *acc m* -litlan, etc.) *adj* short of money, poor

**finna** (finnr; fann, fundu; fundinn) *vb* find, find out; **finna á** *impers* let on, give indication that sth is noticed

**fjár** *n, see* **fé**

**fjǫlmenni** *n* many people, a crowd

**fjǫlmennr** (-menn, -mennt) *adj* with many people; **hversu fjǫlmennr** with how many men

**fjǫr** (-v-) *n* life

**fleiri** *comp adj* more (*see* **margr**)

**flekkr** (-s; -ir) *m* fleck, spot; blot, stain

**forlagðr** *ppart* without or bereft of courage (*from* **leggja**); **verða forlagðr** give up, lose heart, despair

**forverk** *n* humble work, farm

work

**fór** *vb, see* **fara**

**fótr** (*dat* fœti, *gen* fótar; *pl* fœtr, *acc* fœtr) *m* foot; **á fótum** on one's feet; **vera á fótum** be up, afoot, out of bed

**framfœrsla** *f* support, maintenance

**framfœrslumaðr** (*acc* -mann, *dat* -manni, *gen* -manns; *pl* -menn, etc.) *m* pauper

**frá** *prep* [*w dat*] from, about; **segja frá [e-u]** tell about [sth]; *adv* away

**frekr** (frek, frekt) *adj* greedy, eager

**frekt** *n adj as adv* greedily, eagerly (*from* **frekr**)

**fretkarl** (-s; -ar) *m* 'fart-churl', scoundrel

**fretr** *m* fart

**fró** *f* relief, comfort

**fróa** (-að-) *vb* relieve

**frýja** *f* taunt, challenge, reproach

**frýjuorð** *n* taunt, accusation of cowardice

**frændi** (*pl* frændr) *m* kinsman

**fullgoldit** *ppart* fully paid (*from* **gjalda**)

**fylgja** (-ð-) *vb* [*w dat*] follow; back, help, side with, support

**fyrir** *prep* [*w acc/dat*] for; over; **fyrir [e-s] sakar** because of [sth], for the sake of [sth]; **fyrir mínum sǫkum** for my part; **ofan fyrir** [*w acc*] down over; *adv* before (one), present, at hand; ahead, above

**fyrnask** (-ð-) *refl vb* grow old, decay; be forgotten

**fyrri** *comp adj* former

**fœra** (-ð-) *vb* bring, convey; **fœra [e-n] af [e-u]** remove [sth] from [sth]

**fœri** *n* means, occasion, opportunity

**fœri** *vb, see* **fara**

**fǫður** *m, see* **faðir**

**fǫr** (*gen* farar; *pl* farar~farir) *f* journey, trip

## G

**gakk** *2sg imper of* **ganga**

**gamall** (gǫmul, gamalt; *acc m* gamlan, *f* gamla, *dat m* gǫmlum, *n* gǫmlu; *pl* gamlir, etc.; *comp* ellri/eldri, *superl* ellztr/eldstr) *adj* old

**ganga** (gengr; gekk, gengu; genginn) *vb* go, walk

**garðr** (-s; -ar) *m* yard, encosure; fence

**gegnum** *adv* through; **í gegnum** *prep* [*w acc*] through

**gekk** *vb, see* **ganga**

**geldingahǫfuð** *n pl* heads of wethers

**geldingr** (-s; -ar) *m* wether, gelded sheep

**gengi, gengr** *vb, see* **ganga**

**gera** (-ð-) *vb* make, do, act; (*leg*) set the amount of a fine; **gera [e-n] sekan** condemn [sb] to outlawry; **gera til [e-s]** earn [sth]; *refl* **gerask** become, grow to be

**gerðu** = **ger þú**

**gjalda** (geldr; galt, guldu; goldinn) *vb* pay; repay, return

**gjarna** *adv* willingly, gladly; rather

**glœpr** (-s; -ir) *m* crime, misdeed

**goði** *m* chieftain-priest

**góðr** (góð, gott; *comp* betri, *superl* beztr) *adj* good

**gólf** *n* chamber, closet, compartment

**gráta** (grætr; grét, grétu; grátinn) *vb* cry, weep; [*w acc*] bewail, weep for

**gæfa** *f* luck

**gæta** (-tt-) *vb* [*w gen*] watch, take care of, hold

**gørr** *comp adv* more clearly (*from* **gørva**)

**gǫrt** = **gert** *ppart, see* **gera**

**gørva** (*comp* gørr) *adv* quite, clearly

# H

**hafa** (-ð-) *vb* have; take; **hafa verr** fare worse, get the worst of it

**haft** *ppart, see* **hafa**

**hald** (hǫld) *n* support, backing

**halda** (heldr; hélt, héldu; haldinn) *vb* [*w dat*] keep, retain, preserve

**haldkvæmd** *f* convenience, comfort

**hallkvæmr** *adj* fit, fitting, effective, advantageous

**hana** *pron*: *3sg f acc* her (*see* **hon**)

**handsal** (-sǫl) *n* (*usu pl*) (*leg*) handshake deal, bargain, transference of a right or duty to another by joining hands

**hann** (*dat* honum; *pl* þeir) *pron*: *3sg m nom/acc* he, him

**hans** *pron*: *3sg m gen* (of) him (*see* **hann**)

**hans** *poss pron*: *3sg m* his

**happ** (hǫpp) *n* good luck (*with the notion of happenstance*)

**harðfengi** *f* hardihood, valor, vigor

**harmr** (-s; -ar) *m* grief, sorrow

**haust** *n* autumn, fall; **um haustit** in the fall, during the fall

**háls** (háls; hálsar) *m* neck

**hár** (há, hátt; *acc m* hávan; *pl dat* hávum; *comp* hæri, *superl* hæstr) *adj* high, tall

**hefir** *vb, see* **hafa**

**hefna** (-d-) *vb* [*w gen*] avenge, take vengeance

**heill** (heil, heilt) *adj* healthy, well, 'hale'

**heilsa** *f* health

**heim** *adv* home, homewards (*motion*)

**heima** *adv* home, at home (*location*)

**heiman** *adv* from home

**heimskr** *adj* foolish, silly

**heimta** (-t-) *vb* claim (fulfillment of a promise), collect (payment)

**heit** *n* solemn promise, vow

**heita** (heitir; hét, hétu; heitinn) *vb* be named, be called; [*w dat*] promise

**Hel** (-j-) *f* hell, the abode of the dead; death; *also* Hel, goddess of death (*mythological name*)
**heldr** (*superl* helzt) *comp adj* more, rather; **heldr ... en** rather ... than
**heljarmaðr** (*acc* -mann, *dat* -manni, *gen* -manns; *pl* -menn, etc.) *m* powerful, rough man, 'man of Hel'
**helzt** *superl adv* most of all, especially (*from* **heldr**)
**henda** (-d-) *vb* catch; **[e-n] hendir [e-t]** [sb] is caught in, overtaken by [sth] (*as a fault, ill luck, etc.*), [sth] befalls [sb]
**hendi, hendr** *f, see* **hǫnd**
**herað** (heruð~herǫð) *n* district, country
**hestaat** *n* horse-fight
**hestahús** *n* stable
**hestastafr** (-s; -ar~ir) *m* horse-staff (*for use in a horse-fight*)
**hestasveinn** (-s; -ar) *m* horse-boy
**hestaþing** *n* a 'thing' or assembly / meeting for a public horse-fight
**hestr** (-s; -ar) *m* horse, stallion
**hey** *n* hay
**heyra** (-ð-) *vb* hear, listen to
**hér** *adv* here
**hét** *vb, see* **heita**
**hingat** *adv* to here (*motion*), hither
**hitta** (-tt-) *vb* meet
**hjá** *prep* [*w dat*] by, near
**hjó, hjótt** *vb, see* **hǫggva**
**hjóttu = hjótt þú**
**hjuggusk** *vb, see* **hǫggvask**
**hlaupa** (hleypr; hljóp, hljópu; hlaupinn) *vb* leap, jump; **hlaupa at [e-m]** attack [sb]; **hlaupa ofan fyrir** fall down over
**hleypr** *vb, see* **hlaupa**
**hlíf** (-ar) *f* cover, protection (*esp* of a shield or armor)
**hlífarlauss** (-laus, -laust) *adj* uncovered, unprotected, without shield or armor
**hljóp** *vb, see* **hlaupa**
**hluti** *m* part
**hlutr** (*dat* hlut, *gen* -ar; *pl* -ir) *m* share, part; thing; condition, lot
**hlýða** (-dd-) *vb* [*w dat*] listen; **hlýða til** listen to
**Hof** *n* Hof ('Temple') (*place name*)
**hon** (*acc* hana, *dat* henni, *gen* hennar; *pl* þær) *pron*: *3sg f* she
**honum** *pron*: *3sg m dat* (to) him (*see* **hann**)
**horn** *n* horn
**hóll** (hóls; hólar) *m* hill, hillock
**hreysti** *f* valour, prowess
**hross** *n* horse
**hrossahús** *n* stable
**hrossamaðr** (*acc* -mann, *dat* -manni, *gen* -manns; *pl* -menn, etc.) *m* person who knows horses
**hrósa** (-að-) *vb* [*w dat*] boast (of), gloat (over); praise
**hræddr** (hrædd, hrætt) *adj* afraid, frightened, timid; **hræddr við [e-n/e-t]** afraid of [sb/sth]
**hugða, hugði** *vb, see* **hyggja**
**hugr** (*dat* hug(i), *gen* -ar; *pl* -ir) *m* heart, mind, disposition
**hundr** (-s; -ar) *m* dog
**hús** *n* house, building
**húskarl** (-s; -ar) *m* man-servant
**hvar** *int adv* where
**hvarf** *vb, see* **hverfa**

**hvat** *n int pron* what; *rel pron* what, that which (*see* **hverr**)

**hvatti** *vb, see* **hvetja**

**hváptr** (-s; -ar) *m* cheek; mouth

**hvárr** (hvár, hvárt; *acc m* hvárn) *int dual pron* whether; which (of two)

**hvárrtveggi** = **hvárrtveggja**

**hvárrtveggja** *indef dual pron* each (of two); both

**hvárt** *n int pron as adv/conj* whether (or not) (*see* **hvárr**); **hvárt ... eða** *conj* whether ... or

**hvárum tveggja** *see* **hvárrtveggja**

**hverfa** (hverfr; hvarf, hurfu; horfinn) *vb* be lost, disappear

**hvernig** *int adv* how, in what way

**hverr** (hver, hvat; *acc m* -jan) *int pron* who; *adj/indef pron* each, every; everyone

**hversu** *adv* how; **hversu fjǫlmennr** with how many men

**hvert** *adv* to where (*motion*), whither

**hvetja** (hvatt-) *vb* whet, sharpen

**hvé** *int adv* how; to what extent; **hvé nær** when

**hví** *int adv* why, for what (*dat of* **hvat**)

**hvíla** *f* bed

**hvíla** (-ð/d-) *vb* rest, lie, sleep

**hyggja** (hugð-; hug(a)ðr) *vb* think, believe

**hætta** (-tt-) *vb* [*w dat*] leave off, cease; *impers* risk, venture

**hǫfðingi** (-j-) *m* chieftain, leader; captain

**hǫfðingsmaðr** (*acc* -mann, *dat* -manni, *gen* -manns; *pl* -menn, etc.) *m* man of noble extraction or character; generous person

**hǫfðu** *vb, see* **hafa**

**hǫfuð** (*dat* hǫfði; *pl dat* hǫfðum, *gen* hǫfða) *n* head

**hǫfuðbein** *n pl* head-bones

**hǫgg** (-v-) *n* stroke, blow

**høggr** *vb, see* **hǫggva**

**hǫggva** (høggr; hjó, hjoggu/hjuggu; hǫgg(v)inn) *vb* strike, smite; *refl* **hǫggvask** exchange blows, fight; **hǫggvask fyrir** hack away

**hǫnd** (*dat* hendi, *gen* handar; *pl* hendr) *f* hand

## I

**illa** (*comp* verr, *superl* verst) *adv* badly, 'ill'

**illr** (ill, illt; *comp* værri, *superl* verstr) *adj* bad, evil, 'ill'

**inn** *adv* in (*motion*)

**inn** (in, it) *art* the

**innar** *comp adv* farther in (*from* **inn**, *adv*)

## Í

**í** *prep* [*w acc*] in, to, into (*motion*); [*w dat*] in [*position*]

# J

**jafnhár** (-há, -hátt; *acc m* -hávan; *pl dat* -hávum) *adj* as high
**jafnhátt** *n adj as adv* equally, evenly, as high (*from* **jafnhár**)
**jarða** (-að-) *vb* bury
**jól** *n pl* Yule, heathen midwinter festival later applied to Christmas

# K

**kalla** (-að-) *vb* call
**kalls** (*also* kallz) *n* mockery, ridicule
**kann** *vb, see* **kunnu**
**kapítuli** *m* chapter
**kapp** (kǫpp) *n* zeal, eagerness, energy
**kappi** *m* hero, champion
**karl** (-s; -ar) *m* man; old man
**kasta** (-að-) *vb* [*w dat*] throw, cast; *refl* **kastask** cast against one another; **kastask á orðum** exchange words
**kaup** *n* bargain, trade
**kemr** *vb, see* **koma**
**kenna** (-d-) *vb* know, recognize
**kippa** (-t/ð-) *vb* [*w dat*] pull, snatch
**kné** (*dat* kné, *gen* knjés; *pl dat* knjám/knjóm, *gen* knjá) *n* knee
**koma** (kemr~kømr; kom, kómu~kvámu; kominn) *vb* come; **koma á** hit; **koma við [e-t]** touch [sth]; **koma við sǫgur** appear in sagas
**kona** (*pl gen* kvenna) *f* woman
**kómu** *vb, see* **koma**
**kunna** (kann, kunnu; kunni; kunnat) *vb* know; be able to
**kvað** *vb, see* **kveða**
**kveða** (kveðr; kvað, kváðu; kveðinn) *vb* say, state, utter
**kynligr** (-lig, -ligt) *adj* strange, wonderful, extraordinary
**kynsæll** (-sæl, -sælt) *adj* blessed with good and great offspring
**kyrr** (kyrr, kyrrt) *adj* still, calm, quiet
**kǫstuðusk** *vb, see* **kasta**

# L

**lagði**, **lagðisk**, **lagðr** *vb, see* **leggja**
**lamb** (lǫmb) *n* lamb
**lambahǫfuð** *n pl* lambs' heads
**lauss** (laus, laust) *adj* loose, free, unimpeded
**lá** *vb, see* **liggja**
**láta** (lætr; lét, létu; látinn) *vb* put, place, set; let, let on; [*w inf*] have

[sb do sth], cause [sb] to [do sth]

**leggja** (lagð-; *ppart* lag(i)ðr~ laginn) *vb* lay, place, put; [*w dat*] stab, thrust; **leggja at** attack; *refl* **leggjask** lay, set oneself

**leið** (-ir) *f* road, way; **á leið** on the way

**leikr** (*dat* leik, *gen* -s; *pl* -ar) *m* game, play, sport

**leit** *vb, see* **líta**

**leita** (-að-) *vb* [*w gen*] seek, search for

**lengi** *adv* long, for a long time; **opt lengi** too long

**lengr** *comp adv* longer

**letja** (latt-) *vb* hold back, deter, dissuade

**leyfa** (-ð-) *vb* permit, allow

**leyna** (-d-) *vb* hide, conceal; **leyna [e-u] [e-n]** hide [sth] from [sb]

**lét** *vb, see* **láta**

**lifa** (-ð-; *ppart* lifat) *vb* live

**liggja** (liggr; lá, lágu; leginn) *vb* lie, lie down

**líða** (líðr; leið, liðu; liðinn) *vb* pass (by)

**líkligr** (-lig, -ligt; *superl* líkligastr) *adj* likely, probable

**líta** (lítr; leit, litu; litinn) *vb* look, see, behold; **líta á** look at

**lítill** (lítil, lítit; *acc m* lítinn, *f* litla, *dat m* litlum, *n* litlu, *f* lítilli; *pl* litlir, etc.) *adj* little, small; short, brief (*time*); **litlu fyrir** a little before

**lítit** *n adj as indef pron* little (*from* **lítill**)

**ljósta** (lýstr; laust, lustu; lostinn) *vb* strike, hit; **ljósta í svíma** knock unconscious

**lofa** (-að-) *vb* allow, permit

**lok** *n* bolt, lock

**lokhvíla** *f* locked bed-closet

**lostinn** *ppart, see* **ljósta**

**lukka** *f* luck

**lúka** (lýkr; lauk, luku; lokinn) *vb* [*w dat*] close; end, conclude

**lúta** (lýtr; laut, lutu; lotinn) *vb* bow down, bend down

**lýtr** *vb, see* **lúta**

**lægi** *vb, see* **liggja**

**lætr** *vb, see* **láta**

**lœkr** (-jar; -ir) *m* brook, rivulet

**lǫg** *n pl* law, laws

**lǫgsǫgumaðr** (*acc* -mann, *dat* -manni, *gen* -manns; *pl* -menn, etc.) *m* law-speaker

## M

**maðr** (*acc* mann, *dat* manni, *gen* manns; *pl nom/acc* menn, *dat* mǫnnum, *gen* manna) *m* man, person, human being

**maki** *m* match

**makligleikr** (*dat* -leik, *gen* -s; *pl* -ar) *m* (*usu pl*) that which one deserves, serves one right; **at makligleik(a)** deservedly, according to one's just deserts

**makligr** (-lig, -ligt) *adj* fitting, proper, deserving

**mann**, **manna**, **manns** *m, see* **maðr**

**margr** (mǫrg, mar(g)t; *comp* fleiri, *superl* flestr) *adj* [*w sg*] many a (*in collective sense*); [*w pl*] many

**margt** *n adj as indef pron* many a thing (*from* **margr**)

**má** (mái; máði; máðr) *vb* blot out, efface

**má** *vb, see* **mega**

**mál** *n* suit, action, case, matter; **búa mál til** prepare or begin a lawsuit

**mál** *n* meal, mealtime

**mánaðarfró** *f* a month's rest

**mánaðr** (-ar; -ir~r) *m* month

**með** *prep* [*w dat*] with, together with

**meðan** *conj* while, as long as

**mega** (má, megu; mátti; mátt) *aux vb* can, may; *vb* [*w acc*] be able, have strength to accomplish, avail

**meir** *comp adv* more (*see* **mjǫk**)

**meiri** *comp adj* greater; more (*see* **mikill**)

**menn** *m, see* **maðr**

**mestr** *superl adj* greatest, biggest; 'most' (*see* **mikill**)

**meta** (metr; mat, mátu; metinn) *vb* estimate, value; **meta [e-t] við [e-n]** charge [sth] to [sb], leave [sth] for [sb] to do

**mér** *pron*: *1sg dat* (to) me (*see* **ek**)

**mik** *pron*: *1sg acc* me (*see* **ek**)

**mikill** (mikil, mikit; *acc m* mikinn, *f* mikla; *pl* miklir, etc.; *comp* meiri, *superl* mestr) *adj* big, large, great

**mikit** *n adj as adv* greatly, much

**minn** (mín, mitt) *poss adj*: *1sg* my

**mislagðr** *ppart* mislaid (*from* **misleggja**); **[e-m] eru mislagðar hendr í kné** one has 'mislaid hands' upon the knees, does not act when one should

**misleggja** (-lagð-; *ppart* -lag(i)ðr) *vb* lay amiss

**missa** (-t-) *vb* [*w gen*] lose, miss, lack

**mín** *pron*: *1sg gen* of me (*see* **ek**)

**mín**, **mína**, **mínum** *poss adj, see* **mína**

**mjǫk** (*comp* meir(r), *superl* mest) *adv* much

**morginn** (*gen* morgins, *pl* mor(g)nar) *m* morning; **í morgin** this morning; **um morguninn** in the morning

**morgunn** = **morginn**

**móðir** (*acc/dat/gen* móður, *pl* mœðr, *dat* mœðrum, *gen* mœðra) *f* mother

**mót** *n* meeting; **á móti** in return, in exchange

**muntu** = **munt þú**

**munu** (mun, munu; mundi; *pret inf* mundu) *aux vb* will, shall (*futurity*); (*past tense*) would

**myndi**, **myndim** *vb, see* **munu**

**mæla** (-t-) *vb* say, speak; appoint, settle; **mæla til** make arrangement for, initiate, be responsible for; *refl* **mælask** speak, express oneself; **mælask undan** excuse oneself, talk one's way out

**mætta** *vb, see* **mega**

**mǫrgum** *adj see* **margr**

# N

**naut** *n* ox; (*pl*) cattle, oxen
**nefna** (-d-) *vb* name, call
**nenna** (-t-) *vb* have a desire to, be disposed to
**né** *conj* nor
**niðr** *adv* down
**nótt** (*gen* nætr; *pl* nætr) *f* night; **um nóttina** through the night
**nú** *adv* now
**nær** *adv* near; nearly; *conj* when; **hvé nær** when
**nǫkkurr** (nǫkkur, nǫkkut; *acc m* nǫkkurn) *adj/indef pron* one, some, a certain
**nǫkkuru** *adv* somehow, in any way (*from* **nǫkkurr**)
**nǫkkut** *n adj as adv* somewhat (*from* **nǫkkurr**)

# O

**of** *adv* too, too much
**ofan** *adv* down (from above); **ofan fyrir** [*w acc*] down over
**ofmælt** *ppart* spoken in excess, 'overstated' (*from* **mæla**)
**ok** *conj* and (in addition); *adv* also
**okkr** *pron*: *1dual acc/dat* us (two) (*see* **vit**)
**opt** (*comp* optar) *adv* often, frequently; **opt lengi** too long
**optar** *comp adv* more often (*from* **opt**); **eigi optar** not again
**orð** *n* word; **taka til orða** speak up
**orðit** *ppart, see* **verða**
**oss** *pron*: *1pl acc/dat* us (*see* **vér**)

# Ó

**ógipta** *f* ill-luck, haplessness
**ógæfa** *f* ill-luck
**óhapp** *n* ill-luck, mishap
**óhefndr** *ppart* unavenged (*from* **hefna**)
**ójafnaðarmaðr** (*acc* -mann, *dat* -manni, *gen* -manns; *pl* -menn, etc.) *m* unjust man, one who is quarrelsome and overbearing, difficult to deal with
**ómegð** *f* the state of being dependent; (*coll*) those who are unable to support themselves
**ómerkr** (ómerk, ómerkt) *adj* insignificant, silly
**ór** *prep* [*w dat*] out of, from
**ósœmð** *f* disgrace, dishonor
**óvanari** *comp adj* less accustomed (*from* **vanr**)

## P

**prestr** (-s; -ar) *m* priest

## R

**ragr** (rǫg, ragt) *adj* cowardly
**rann** *vb, see* **renna**
**Rannveig** *f* Rannveig (*personal name*)
**rauðavíkingr** (-s; -ar) *m* 'red' viking, a particularly fierce and violent viking
**rauðr** (rauð, rautt) *adj* red
**ráða** (ræðr; réð, réðu; ráðinn) *vb* advise; decide, have one's way; **ef ek má ráða** if I can have it as I like
**reið** (-ar) *f* ride, act of riding (a horse)
**reiðhestr** (-s; -ar) *m* riding-horse (*as distinct from a pack-horse*)
**rekkja** *f* bed
**rekkjugólf** *n* a bed-closet
**renna** (rennr; rann, runnu; runninn) *vb* run, flee; **[e-t] rennr [e-m] í skap** *impers* [sb] takes [sth] to heart, is much affected by [sth]
**rista** (-t-) *vb* cut, scratch
**ríða** (ríðr; reið, riðu; riðinn) *vb* ride, go on horseback
**ríkari** *comp adj, see* **ríkr**
**ríki** *n* realm, kingdom; power
**ríkismaðr** (*acc* -mann, *dat* -manni, *gen* -manns; *pl* -menn, etc.) *m* man of power
**ríkr** (rík, ríkt; *acc m* -jan; *comp* -ari) *adj* strong, powerful
**rísa** (ríss; reis, risu; risinn) *vb* arise, rise, stand up; **rísa upp** rise up, get up
**Rómaborg** *f* the city of Rome (*place name*)
**runnit** *ppart, see* **renna**
**rœða** (-dd-) *vb* speak, chat, gossip

## S

**saga** *f* story, saga
**sagði, sagt** *vb, see* **segja**
**sakar** *f, see* **sǫk**
**saklauss** (-laus, -laust) *adj* innocent
**sal** (sǫl) *n* bargain, sale
**saman** *adv* together
**samheraðs** *adv* within the same district
**samr** (sǫm, samt) *adj* same
**sannr** (sǫnn, satt) *adj* true
**sat** *vb, see* **sitja**

**satt** *adj, see* **sannr**
**sax** (sǫx) *n* short sword
**sá** (sú, þat; *pl* þeir) *dem pron* that (one)
**sá** *vb, see* **sjá**
**sár** *n* wound
**sátu** *vb, see* **sitja**
**segja** (sagð-) *vb* say, tell; **segja af** tell about; **segja frá** tell about; **segja til sín** give one's name, identify oneself
**seinn** (sein, seint) *adj* slow
**seint** *n adj as adv* slowly, at a slow pace (*from* **seinn**)
**sekr** (sek, sekt) *adj* convicted, condemned, outlawed
**selja** (-d-) *vb* sell; **selja undan** sell off
**sem** *rel pron* which, that (= **er**); *conj* as, like; as if
**senda** (-d-) *vb* send
**sé** *vb, see* **sjá**
**sé** *vb, see* **vera**
**sér** *refl pron*: *dat* (to) him-/her-/it-/oneself, themselves (*see* **sik**)
**sik** (*dat* sér, *gen* sín) *refl pron*: *acc* him-/her-/it-/oneself
**sinn** *n* a time, instance; **sitt sinn** in turn
**sinn** (sín, sitt) *refl poss adj* his, her, its, their (own)
**sitja** (sitr; sat, sátu; setinn) *vb* sit; stay
**sitt** *refl poss adj, see* **sinn**
**síð** (*comp* síðar) *adv* late
**síðan** *adv* then, after that
**síðar** *comp adv* later, afterwards
**síðastr** *superl adj* last
**síðr** (síð, sítt) *adj* long, hanging
**sín** *refl pron*: *gen* (of) him-/her-/it-/oneself, themselves (*see* **sik**)
**sína, síns, sínu, sínum** *refl poss adj, see* **sinn**
**sjá** (sér; sá, sá(u); sénn) *vb* see
**sjálfbjargi** *adj indecl* self-sufficing, self-helpful
**sjálfr** (sjálf, sjálft) *adj* (my-/your-/him-/her-/it-/one-)self
**sjón** *f* sight, eyesight
**sjónlauss** (-laus, -laust) *adj* blind
**sjónlítill** (-lítil, -lítit; *acc m* -litlan, etc.) *adj* having poor eyesight
**skal, skalt** *vb, see* **skulu**
**skaltu** = **skalt þú**
**skammr** (skǫmm, skam(m)t; *comp* skemri, *superl* skemstr) *adj* short, brief
**skammt** *n adj as adv* a short distance, not far (*from* **skammr**)
**skap** (skǫp) *n* condition of mind, temper, mood; **[e-t] rennr [e-m] í skap** *impers* [sb] takes [sth] to heart, is much affected by [sth]
**skelfr** *vb, see* **skjálfa**
**skilja** (-d/ð-, *ppart* skiliðr~skildr~skilinn) *vb* part, separate, divide; **skiliðr við** parted from, separated from
**skip** *n* ship
**skipta** (-t-) *vb* [*w dat*] divide, share, deal out; **skipta með [e-m]** exchange with [sb]
**skjálfa** (skelfr; skalf, skulfu; skolfinn) *vb* shiver, shake, quiver
**skjǫldr** (*dat* skildi, *gen* skjaldar; *pl* skildir, *acc* skjǫldu) *m* shield
**skoltr** (-s; -ar) *m* jaw, snout (of an animal)
**skógarmaðr** (*acc* -mann, *dat* -manni, *gen* -manns; *pl* -menn,

etc.) *m* outlaw, 'woods-man'
**skógr** (-ar; -ar) *m* forest, woods
**skór** (*dat* skó, *gen* skós; *pl* skúar~skór, *acc* skúa, *dat* skóm, *gen* skúa) *m* shoe
**skóþvengr** (-jar; -ir) *m* 'shoe-thong', shoe-string
**skrautligr** *adj* splendid
**skulu** (skal, skulu; skyldi; *pret inf* skyldu) *aux vb* shall (*obligation, purpose, necessity, fate*); (*past tense*) should
**skyldi**, **skyldu** *vb, see* **skulu**
**skyrta** *f* shirt
**skyrtublað** (-blǫð) *n* shirt-lap
**skǫruligast** *n adj as adv* bravely, boldly (*from superl of* **skǫruligr**); **sem skǫruligast** as bravely as possible
**skǫruligr** (-lig, -ligt; *superl* skǫruligastr) *adj* brave, bold, manly
**slíkr** (slík, slíkt) *adj* such; like; **slíkr sem** such as, similar to
**slíta** (slítr; sleit, slitu; slitinn) *vb* [*w dat*] rend, tear; wear out (*of clothes*)
**sljóvgask** *refl vb* grow slow, dull, blunt (*of a sword*)
**smár** (smá, smátt; *acc m* smán, *f* smá, *dat m* smám, *n* smá; *pl f* smár; *comp* smæri, *superl* smæstr) *adj* small, little
**smæri** *comp adj* smaller (*from* **smár**)
**snarligr** (-lig, -ligt; *comp* -ligri) *adj* keen, quick
**snimma** *adv* early
**sofa** (sefr; svaf, sváfu; sofinn) *vb* sleep; **sofa af (um nóttina)** sleep through the night
**sonardauðr** (*gen* -ar) *m* death of a son
**sonr** (*dat* syni, *gen* sonar; *pl* synir, *acc* sonu) *m* son
**spara** (-ð-; *ppart* spar(a)ðr) *vb* spare; **spara [e-t] við sik** spare oneself from, shrink from [sth]
**spurði** *vb, see* **spyrja**
**spyrja** (spurð-) *vb* ask
**staðr** (*dat* stað(i), *gen* -ar; *pl* -ir) *m* place, stead; **í [e-s] stað** in place of [sb/sth]
**stafr** (-s; -ar~ir) *m* staff, stick
**stakk** *vb, see* **stinga**
**standa** (stendr; stóð, stóðu; staðinn) *vb* stand
**stanga** (-að-) *vb* poke, goad; butt, gore (*of cattle*)
**stangarhǫgg** *n* staff-struck
**stendr** *vb, see* **standa**
**sté** *vb, see* **stíga**
**stilltr** (stillt, stillt) *adj* calm, even-tempered
**stinga** (stingr; stakk, stungu; stunginn) *vb* thrust, stick, stab; **stinga hendi við [ẹ-m]** shove [sb] with the hand or arm
**stíga** (stígr; steig/sté, stigu; stiginn) *vb* step, tread, walk; **stíga undan borði** get up from the table
**stoða** (-að-) *vb* avail, be of use
**stóð** *vb, see* **standa**
**stóðhross** *n* stud-horse
**stórr** (stór, stórt; *comp* stœrri, *superl* stœrstr) *adj* big, great; powerful
**stund** (*dat* -u; *pl* -ir) *f* a while, a certain length of time; **á annarri stundu ... á annarri** at one time

... at another, now ... then; **um stundar sakar** for a while

**stǫng** (*gen* stangar; *pl* stangir/ stengr) *f* pole, staff

**suðr** *adv* southwards

**sumar** (*dat* sumri; *pl* sumur, *dat* sumrum, *gen* sumra) *n* summer

**sunna** *f* sun

**Sunnudalr** (*dat* -dal, *gen* -dals) *m* Sunnudal ('South Dale', 'South Valley', *or perh* 'Sun Dale') (*place name*)

**sú** (*dat* þeiri; *pl* þær) *dem pron*: *f sg* that (one) (*see* **sá**)

**svara** (-að-) *vb* [*w dat*] answer, reply; **svara [e-m] [e-u]** to answer [sth] to [sb]

**svá** *adv* so, thus, such; **svá at (svá ... at)** so that, such that, in such a way that

**svefn** (*gen* svefns) *m* sleep; **fara til svefns** go to sleep

**sveinn** (-s; -ar) *m* boy; servant, attendant

**sverð** *n* sword

**sviðueldr** (-s; -ar) *m* fire for roasting sheep's heads

**svíða** (svíðr; sveið, sviðu; sviðinn) *vb* burn, singe

**svíkja** (svíkr; sveik, sviku; svikinn) *vb* betray

**svími** *m* swoon; **ljósta í svíma** knock unconscious

**svǫruðu** *vb*, *see* **svara**

**syni** *m*, *see* **sonr**

**sýna** (-d-) *vb* show; *refl* **sýnask** seem, appear; *impers* [*w dat*] seem [to sb]; seem fitting [to sb]

**sýta** (-t-) *vb* wail, lament, mourn for

**sæng** (*gen* sæng(a)r; *pl* sængr) *f* bed

**sæti** *vb*, *see* **sitja**

**sǫgðu**, **sǫgðusk** *vb*, *see* **segja**

**sǫgur** *f*, *see* **saga**

**sǫk** (*gen* sakar; *pl* sakar/sakir) *f* cause, reason, 'sake'; **fyrir [e-s] sakar** because of [sth], for the sake of [sth]; **fyrir mínum sǫkum** for my part; **um stundar sakar** for a while

## T

**taka** (tekr; tók, tóku; tekinn) *vb* take, take hold of, grasp; **taka [e-t] frá [e-m]** take [sth] from [sb], deprive [sb] of [sth]; **taka í hǫnd** take by the hand; **taka til [e-s]** concern [sth]; **taka til at** [*w inf*] begin to [do sth]; **taka til orða** begin to speak, speak up

**tal** (tǫl) *n* talk, conversation

**tala** (-að-) *vb* talk, speak

**taumr** (-s; -ar) *m* rein

**tekr** *vb*, *see* **taka**

**til** *prep* [*w gen*] to, for; until; **til þess er** *conj* until

**tilræði** *n* assault (with a weapon); **veita [e-m] tilræði** make an assault on [sb]

**tíðast** *n adj as adv* most commonly; most widely spoken (*from* **tíðastr**)

**tíðastr** *superl adj* most common; most widely spoken of (*from* **tíðr**)

**tíðendi** *n pl* news, tidings

**tíðr** (tíð, títt; *superl* tíðastr) *adj* frequent; usual; often spoken of; **hvat var títt** what had happened

**toga** (-að-) *vb* draw, tug, pull

**tók, tókum** *vb, see* **taka**

**troll** *n* troll

**trúmaðr** (*acc* -mann, *dat* -manni, *gen* -manns; *pl* -menn, etc.) *m* true believer, good Christian

**trúr** (trú, trútt) *adj* faithful, true, loyal; believing; safe; **eigi trútt, at...** it is not true, safe to say that...

**tunga** *f* tongue

**tún** *n* home-field, i.e., the enclosed field in front of a homestead; also, a farmhouse and its buildings

**tvá** *num, see* **tveir**

**tveir** (*acc m* tvá) *num* two

# U

**um** *prep* [*w acc*] about, in regard to; during, in (*time*)

**una** (-ð/d-) *vb* [*w dat*] love; be content with, enjoy

**undan** *prep* [*w dat*] from under; away from; *adv* away; **selja undan** sell off

**undir** *prep* [*w acc*] under, underneath (*motion*); [*w dat*] under, underneath (*location*)

**ungr** (ung, ungt) *adj* young

**unz** *conj* until

**upp** *adv* up (*motion*)

**uppaustr** (*gen* -rar) *m* a scooping up

**uppaustrarmaðr** (*acc* -mann, *dat* -manni, *gen* -manns; *pl* -menn, etc.) *m* a gossip, babbler (*from* **uppaustr**)

**uxi** (*pl* [*often irregularly n*] yxn~øxn, *dat* yxnum~øxnum, *gen* yxna~øxna> *m* ox

# Ú

**út** *adv* out (*motion*)

**útan** *adv* abroad, away from Iceland (usu. denoting Norway)

**úti** *adv* out (*location*), outside

# V

**vakði** *vb, see* **vekja**

**vakna** (-að-) *vb* awaken, wake up

**vald** (vǫld) *n* power, might, authority

**van-** *pref* under-, un-, prefix denoting lack

**vandr** (vǫnd, vant) *adj* hard, difficult; **allt vandr** altogether difficult

**vanheilsa** *f* poor health, illness

**vann** *vb, see* **vinna**

**vanr** (vǫn, vant; *comp* vanari) *adj* accustomed, usual, wont; **vera vanr [e-u]** be accustomed to [sth]

**vanr** (vǫn, vant) *adj* [*w gen*] lacking, wanting; **einskis vanr** lacking nothing

**vant** *adj, see* **vandr**

**var, vart** *vb, see* **vera**

**vara** (-ð-) *vb impers* [*w gen of thing, acc of person*] expect

**varð** *vb, see* **verða**

**varðisk** *vb, see* **verja**

**varðveita** (-tt-) *vb* keep, take care of

**varliga** *adv* warily, carefully

**varnaðr** (*gen* -ar) *m* warning, caution

**vartu = vart þú**

**Vateri** *m* Vateri (*place name*)

**váðaverk** *n* (*leg*) accidental deed, of harm inflicted unintentionally

**ván** (-ir) *f* hope, expectation

**vápn** *n* weapon

**vápnskipti** *n* exchange of weapons; exchange of blows

**várr** (vár, várt) *poss adj*: *1pl* our

**váru** *vb, see* **vera**

**vega** (vegr; vá, vágu; veginn) *vb* kill, slay

**veggr** (-jar~s; -ir) *m* wall

**vegit** *ppart of* **vega**

**veita** (-tt-) *vb* grant, give; help, assist; allow, permit; **veita [e-m] tilræði** make an assault on [sb]; **veitir þungt við [e-n]** it proves difficult to deal with [sb]

**vekja** (vakð-, *ppart* vakiðr~vaktr~vakinn) *vb* waken [sb], rouse from sleep (*trans*)

**vel** *adv* well, very

**vera** (er; var, váru; verit) *vb* be; stay

**verða** (verðr; varð, urðu; orðinn) *vb* become; happen, come to pass; [*w inf*] must (*necessity*); **verða at** become; happen, come about; **verða fyrir [e-u]** meet with [sth]; **verðr þú nær at ganga** you must come near

**verðr** (verð, vert) *adj* worth, worthy, deserving

**verja** (varð-, var(i)ðr) *vb* defend; *refl* **verjask** defend oneself

**verk** *n* work, deed

**verr** *comp adv* worse (*see* **illa**)

**verri** *comp adj* worse (*see* **illr**)

**vetr** (vetrar; vetr) *m* winter; **um vetrinn** in, during the winter

**vér** (*acc/dat* oss) *pron*: *1pl* we (*see* **ek**)

**við** *prep* [*w acc*] by, close to; with, against

**vili** (-j-) *m* will, wish

**vilja** (vill; vildi; viljat) *vb* wish, want

**vinna** (vinnr; vann, unnu; unninn) *vb* work, perform, labor

**vinr** (-ar; -ir) *m* friend

**vinsæll** (-sæl, -sælt; *comp* -sælli) *adj* popular, blessed with friends

**vinsælli** *comp adj* more popular, better liked (*from* **vinsæll**)

**virða** (-ð-) *vb* consider, value, estimate the worth of

**virðing** (-ar) *f* value, worth; reputation, honor

**vist** (-ir) *f* stay; lodging; **á vist** lodging, staying (at one's house)

**vit** (*acc/dat* okkr) *pron*: *1dual* we (two) (*see* **ek**)

**vit** *n* good sense, wit, intelligence

**vita** (veit, vitu; vissi; vitaðr) *vb* know, understand

**víða** *adv* widely, far and wide, in many places

**víg** *n* fight, battle; killing; (*leg*) homicide, manslaughter

**vígkœnn** (-kœn, -kœnt) *adj* skillful in fighting, 'battle-keen'

**víkingr** (-s; -ar) *m* viking, sea-raider

**vísa** (-að-) *vb* show, point out, indicate; **vísa [e-m] til [e-s]** show, point out [to sb] [sth]; **vísa [e-m] á leið** point [sb] on the way

**víss** (vís, víst) *adj* certain; wise; **at vísu** certainly, of course

**víst** *n adj as adv* certainly, for sure (*from* **víss**)

**víti** *n* fine, punishment

**vægja** (-ð-) *vb* [*w dat*] spare

**vænn** (væn, vænt) *adj* promising, likely, to be expected; **þykkir [e-m] eigi vænt til [e-s]** [sb] is not confident of [sth]

**væri** *vb*, *see* **vera**

## Y

**yðarr** (yður, yðart; *pl n* yður) *poss adj*: *2pl* your

**yður** *poss adj*, *see* **yðarr**

**yfir** *adv* over

**ykkr** *pron*: *2dual acc/dat* you (two) (*see* **þit**)

## Þ

**þaðan** *adv* from there

**þagat** *ppart*, *see* **þegja**

**þar** *adv* there, at that point; **þar sem** *conj* where

**þat** (*dat* því, *gen* þess; *pl* þau) *dem pron*: *n nom/acc* that (one) (*see* **sá**)

**þau** (*dat* þeim, *gen* þeira) *pron*: *3pl n nom/acc* they, them (*n*, *mixed*)

**þá** *pron*: *3pl m acc* them (*see* **þeir**)

**þá** *adv* then; **þá er** *conj* when

**þáttr** (*dat* þætti, *gen* þáttar, *pl* þættir, *acc* þáttu) *m* short story, tale

**þegar** *adv* immediately; *conj* as soon as; **þegar er** as soon as

**þegja** (þagð-, *ppart* þagat) *vb* be silent; be quiet

**þeim** *pron*: *3pl dat* them (*see*

**þeir**)

**þeir** (*acc* þá, *dat* þeim, *gen* þeira) *pron*: *3pl m* they

**þeir** (þær, þau) *dem pron*: *pl m* those (*see* **sá**)

**þeira** *poss pron*: *3pl* their

**þeiri** *dem pron, see* **sú**

**þenna** *dem pron, see* **þessi**

**þess** *dem pron, see* **þat**

**þessa**, **þessu**, **þessum** *dem pron, see* **þessi**

**þessi** (*n* þetta; *acc m* þenna, *dat m* þessum, *n* þessu, *gen m/n* þessa; *pl n* þessi) *dem pron*: *sg m/f* this (one)

**þetta** *dem pron, see* **þessi**

**þér** *pron*: *2sg dat* (to) you (*see* **þú**)

**þér** (*acc/dat* yðr, *gen* yðar) *pron*: *2 pl* you

**þik** *pron*: *2sg acc* you (*see* **þú**)

**þing** *n* assembly

**þingmaðr** (*acc* -mann, *dat* -manni, *gen* -manns; *pl* -menn, etc.) *m* liegeman of a particular chieftain

**þinn** (þín, þitt) *poss adj*: *2sg* your

**þit** (*acc/dat* ykkr) *pron*: *2dual* you (two) (*see* **þú**)

**þín** *pron*: *2sg gen* of you (*see* **þú**)

**þín**, **þína**, **þíns**, **þínu**, **þínum** *poss adj, see* **þinn**

**þola** (-ð-; *ppart* þol(a)t) *vb* suffer, endure, bear; **þola [e-t] [e-m]** endure [sth] from [sb]

**Þorsteinn** (-s) *m* Thorstein (*personal name*)

**Þorvaldr** (-s) *m* Thorvald (*personal name*)

**þó** *adv* yet, nevertheless

**Þórarinn** (-s) *m* Thorarin (*personal name*)

**Þórðr** (-ar) *m* Thord (*personal name*)

**Þórhallr** (-s) *m* Thorhall (*personal name*)

**þótt** = **þó at** *conj* [*w subjunct*] although, even though

**þótti** *vb, see* **þykkja**

**þraut** (-ir) *f* struggle, great exertion

**þrautbeztr** *superl adj* best in struggles, most persevering (*see* **þrautgóðr**)

**þrautgóðr** (-góð, -gott) *adj* persevering, steadfast in difficulties

**þrek** *n* strength, courage, fortitude; **hafa þrek til [e-s]** have the courage to do [sth]

**þriggja** *num, see* **þrír**

**þrír** (*acc* þrjá, *gen* þriggja) *num* three

**þrjá** *num, see* **þrír**

**þræll** (þræls; þrælar) *m* bondservant, slave, thrall

**þukla** (-að-) *vb* grope, feel, touch; **þukla á [e-u]** grope for [sth]

**þungr** (þung, þungt) *adj* heavy; oppressive; weighty

**þurfa** (þarf, þurfu; þurfti; þurft) *vb* [*w gen*] need, have need of

**þú** (*acc* þik, *dat* þér, *gen* þín; *dual* þit; *pl* þér) *pron*: *2sg* you

**þvengr** (-jar; -ir) *m* thong

**því** *dat of* **þat**; *as adv* therefore, for that reason; [*w comp*] the (more); **því vinsælli** the better liked, the more popular; **því at** *conj* because

**þykkja** (þykkir; þótti; þótt) *vb*

*impers* [*w dat*] seem [to sb]; *refl* **þykkjask** consider oneself

**þyrsta** (-t-) *vb impers* [*w acc*] be thirsty; **þyrstir mik** I am thirsty

**þær** *dem pron*: *f pl* those (*see* **sú**)

## Æ

**ætla** (-að-) *vb* think, expect, suppose; intend, purpose, mean

**ævi** *f* age, time

## Œ

**œpa** (-ð-) *vb* cry out, shout

**œska** *f* youth, childhood

## Ǫ/Ø

**ǫðru**, **ǫðrum** *adj*, *see* **annarr**

**ǫflugr** (ǫflug, ǫflugt) *adj* strong, powerful

**ǫllu** *adj*, *see* **allr**

**ǫndvegi** *n* high-seat, seat of honor; **sitja í ǫðru ǫndvegi** sit in the second high-seat, the next-highest seat of honor

**ørendlaust** *adv* without purpose, in vain, for nothing; **fara ørend-laust** go in vain

**ǫttu** *vb*, *see* **etja**

**øx** (*acc/dat* -i; *pl* -ar) *f* ax

# FURTHER SUGGESTED READINGS

## THE VIKING LANGUAGE SERIES

Modern introductions to Old Norse language, runes, and Icelandic sagas, with viking history and literature

***Viking Language 1: Learn Old Norse, Runes and Icelandic Sagas*** (2nd Edition) is a new introduction to Old Norse, Icelandic sagas, and runes. Requires no previous language knowledge. Everything from beginner to advanced in one book: graded lessons, vocabulary, grammar exercises, pronunciation, and extensive maps. Includes sections on Viking history, literature, and myth. Innovative word-frequency method greatly speeds learning. Modern Icelandic has changed little from Old Norse and students are well on the way to mastering Modern Icelandic. **Free Answer Key** to the exercises in *Viking Language 1* on our website www.oldnorse.org

***Viking Language 2: The Old Norse Reader*** is a treasure trove of Scandinavian lore. It offers a wide variety of Old Norse sources and runes and contains a large vocabulary, chapters on eddic and skaldic poetry, and a full reference grammar. (The latter, invaluable for learning to read sagas.) The reader also includes myths, legends, and runic inscriptions about Scandinavian gods, vikings, monster-slayers, dwarves, giants, warrior kings, and valkyries.

### PRONOUNCIATION ALBUMS for *Viking Language 1*

Two MP3 Albums, **Audio Lessons 1-8 and Audio Lessons 9-15,** teach the pronunciation of saga passages and runes in *Viking Language 1*. The pronunciation is a slightly archaic modern Icelandic as used in the saga and language courses at the University of Iceland. Both albums are available for download and purchase on our website www.oldnorse.org and on Amazon and iTunes.

For more information visit our website www.oldnorse.org

## THE ICELANDIC SAGA SERIES

### New English dual-language translations with the original Old Norse text, vocabulary, introductions, maps, and notes

***The Tale of Thorstein Staff Struck* (*Þorsteins þáttr stangarhǫggs*)** is a short saga set in Iceland's East Fjords during the 10th-century Viking Age. Thorstein, a peaceful young man, is forced to live with the humiliating nickname "staff struck." Even Thorstein's father, an old Viking, looks down on his son as a coward. But Thorstein is no coward. Waiting for the right moment to take revenge, Thorstein reclaims his good name in a way that brings honor both to him and his chieftain.

***Saga of the People of Weapon's Fjord* (*Vápnfirðinga saga*)** is a classic Icelandic saga of feuding chieftains struggling for power and survival. Set during the Viking Age in Iceland's East Fjords, the saga recounts how a rich Norwegian merchant stirs the greed of the local Icelanders. Sons avenge fathers, while wives and mothers demand honor for their families. This new edition opens for the modern reader a lost world in the far North Atlantic.

## COMING SOON

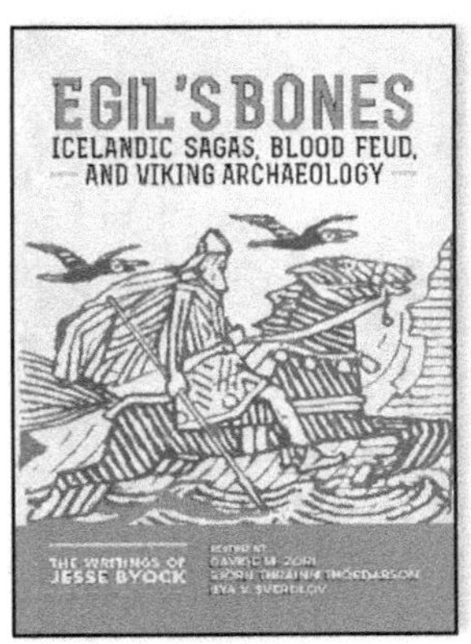


***Egil's Bones: Icelandic Sagas, Blood Feud, and Viking Archaeology*** by Jesse Byock explores Viking Age Iceland: its origins, sagas, heroes, society, and archaeology. The book provides a comprehensive picture of an unusual North Atlantic community steeped in the lore of the past. You will explore the background of legendary heroes such as Sigurd the dragon slayer, whose saga influenced J.R.R. Tolkien and Richard Wagner. So also, consider the archaeological bones of the Viking warrior poet, Egil Skalla-Grimsson. Edited by Davide Zori, Björn Þráinn Þórðarson, and Ilya Sverdlov.

## ADDITIONAL RESOURCES

***Viking Age Iceland*** combines anthropology, archaeology, and history. It offers crucial insights into the Icelandic sagas and the inner workings of a feuding society. Unusual for Western Europe, Iceland had no king, no foreign policy, and no defense forces and shows intriguing proto-democratic tendencies. It should have been a utopia, yet its sagas are dominated by blood feud, killings, and the search for peace. In exploring the processes of conflict and peace-making this study has broad implications for the international study of feud and conflict.

***Feud in the Icelandic Saga*** explores conflicts at the core of Iceland's sagas. Jesse Byock shows how the dominant concern of medieval society was the channeling of violence into accepted patterns of feud and the regulation of conflict. The sometimes conflicting demands of blood feud and honor are explored. This wide-ranging study also considers the narrative structure and oral background of the sagas and the role of these stories in a Viking heritage society in the far North Atlantic.

www.ingramcontent.com/pod-product-compliance
Lightning Source LLC
Chambersburg PA
CBHW071950190726
48293CB00004B/1416